THE COMPANION TO THE PBS TELEVISION SERIES
HOSTED BY MARCUS SAMUELSSON

THE MEANING OF
FOOD

PATRICIA HARRIS, DAVID LYON,
AND SUE McLAUGHLIN

The
Globe
Pequot
Press

GUILFORD, CONNECTICUT

The authors gratefully acknowledge the contributions of Susan Kim, writer for *The Meaning of Food* PBS series, whose work was referenced in the writing of this book.

Text design by LeAnna Weller Smith

Photo credits: pp. vii (top left), x (right), xii, 4 (left), 8 (right), 9, 29 (top right), 29 (bottom), 32, 51 (right), 71 (left), 83, 84 (left), 84–85 (hams), 86, 99, 109–10, 113, 117, 122–24, 125 (left), 132–33 (stars), 134, 139: Getty; pp. iv, vii (bottom), 3, 4 (right), 7, 10–11, 13 (left), 18, 20–21, 24 (right), 26–27, 33 (right), 34, 37 (left), 38, 45 (right), 47 (left), 49, 52, 57–60, 63–64, 68–69, 71 (right), 72, 75 (right), 76 (left), 80 (left), 88–89, 90 (right), 91 (right), 94–95, 96–97 (coconut), 97 (right), 98, 100, 102–3, 106, 114, 125 (right), 128–31, 132 (left), 136 (left), 142 (left), 145–46, 154–55 (glasses), 164: photography by Liesa Cole/ photo styling by Lea Wolf; pp. iii, vii (top right), x (left), 8 (left), 16, 22, 33 (left), 42 (left), 56, 115: PhotoDisk®; pp. xi, 5, 13 (right), 29 (top left), 41, 42 (right), 45 (left), 50–51 (dragon), 53, 75 (left), 79, 90 (left), 91 (left), 104, 118–19, 133 (right), 135, 149, 163: Photos.com; pp. viii, 17, 24 (left), 25 (top row), 30–31, 44, 54, 66 (left), 67 (right), 80 (right), 80 (center), 81, 82 (left), 82 (right), 87, 93, 101 (right), 111, 120 (left), 126–27, 137 (right), 140–41, 142 (right), 143, 152, 154 (left), 155 (right), 157: Pie in the Sky Productions

Video captures: p. 82 (center): © KOMO TV, Seattle; pp. ix, 14–15, 19, 25 (bottom), 36, 37 (right), 47 (right), 48, 55, 66 (right), 67 (left), 76 (right), 77, 92, 101 (left), 120 (right), 121, 136 (right), 137 (left), 150–51: Pie in the Sky Productions

Library of Congress Cataloging-in-Publication Data
Harris, Patricia, 1949-
    The meaning of food : the companion to the PBS television series / Patricia Harris, David Lyon, and Sue McLaughlin.—
1st ed.
        p. cm.
    Includes bibliographical references and index.
    ISBN 0-7627-3837-5
    1. Food habits—Social aspects—United States. 2. Ethnic food industry—United States. I. Lyon, David, 1949- II. McLaughlin, Sue. III. Meaning of food (Television program) IV. Title.

GT2853.U5H64 2005
349.1'2—dc22   2004060804

Manufactured in the United States of America
First Edition/First Printing

TO BILLIE AND JOHN, WHO FED ME.
—S. McLAUGHLIN

CONTENTS

"Food is our common ground, a universal experience."
—James Beard

No matter who we are or where we live on this planet, all life revolves around food. Yet food is more than the sustenance we need to stay alive; it is part of our culture and tradition and can be the very thing that defines us as a people. Food has the power to create relationships, change perspectives, and take us places we never thought possible.

It is through food that we create moments of togetherness; through food that we express ourselves; through food that we share times of celebration and sorrow; and through food that we mark the changing seasons and the passing of time. Food adds creativity to our days and excitement to our nights. It nourishes our minds, our bodies, and our souls.

No matter where we are from, how we cook, or what we enjoy, food enriches our lives in special moments and in the everyday.

The Meaning of Food gratefully acknowledges the support of Knorr®, a proud and longstanding contributor to the culture of food throughout the world. So please join us as we take you on a worldwide journey exploring the many ways in which food adds flavor to our lives.

Major funding for The Meaning of Food *was provided by Unilever. Additional funding was provided by Pacific Islanders in Communications, Humanities Washington Documentary Pooled Fund, the Corporation for Public Broadcasting, and PBS.*

Knorr is a registered trademark of the Unilever group of companies.

PREFACE

The Meaning of Food was conceived more than a decade ago. At the time, I was traveling in Africa, the Middle East, and Mexico, working on another PBS documentary project that looked at various cultures' attitudes toward death. I had never before traveled so extensively, and in such a concentrated period of time. When I had a moment to reflect back on my journeys, I realized with surprise that even though we were meeting and interviewing individuals around one of the most elemental, emotional, and affecting topics possible—death—the times I felt I really got to see inside people's lives and hearts were instead over food: sampling their beloved specialties, asking questions about ingredients and methods, simply breaking bread together. I ate homemade moussaka for Easter with a Palestinian Christian family and, much to the delight of all gathered, joined the children in eating what I hope were raw almonds—called lauz—off the ground. In Ghana I visited the home of our van driver to meet his wife and to sample fufu (pounded yams) served with goat (or perhaps it was bush pig?), and kenkey (a kind of fermented corn) cooked with greens and pepper sauce.

Even when I returned from my travels, food remained the focus. The questions my family and friends most often asked were: "What do they eat there?" "Did you try it?" "How did you get out of having to try it?" and "Couldn't you find any _____ [insert comfort food of choice from the United States]?"

It was then that I first began to think more about the meaning of food.

Like all animals, we eat to survive. But as humans, we transform simple *feeding* into the ritual art of *dining*, creating customs and rites that turn out to be as crucial to our well-being as are proteins and carbohydrates. This is because everything about eating—including what we consume, how we acquire it, who prepares it, and who's at the table—is a form of communication rich with meaning. Our attitudes, practices, and rituals around food are a window onto our most basic beliefs about our world and ourselves.

Heavy stuff. I was convinced the topic would make for a fascinating documentary, and set about busily reading and researching. At first I thought the series should be internationally focused, but I soon

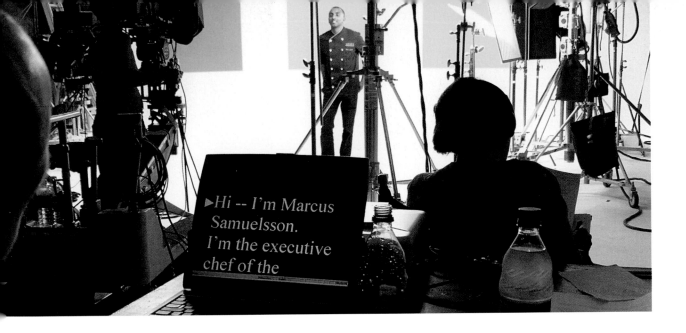

realized that concentrating on the United States, with our rich amalgam of peoples and cultures, would be just as illuminating. And I quickly discovered that my personal epiphany about the importance of food was old hat to anthropologists. Researching a group's "foodways" turns out to be one of the oldest tricks in the book for finding out what makes them tick.

But, interestingly enough, it appeared that this awareness of the intense connection between food and culture didn't resonate with many Americans. It was difficult to get people to understand that the series would not be a cooking show, nor a history of specific ingredients, nor a compendium of food festivals. Instead it would be a collection of stories about people whose food and eating habits revealed important things about them. Anthropologists got the concept immediately, as did people from other countries. People from Hawai`i (a place singularly defined by its crazy mix of cultures and food traditions) got it, but many mainlanders didn't. Apparently we've become so focused on the physical details of what we're eating—how it tastes, what it's made of, how many calories or carbohydrates it has—that

we've forgotten about the crucial act of *dining:* whom we're eating with and why.

And so *The Meaning of Food* was born. It's a subject near and dear to me and to Marcus Samuelsson, the host of our three-part PBS series. An Ethiopian by birth, Swede by adoption, and now a New Yorker by choice, Marcus is the perfect person to serve as master of ceremonies for this project. The renowned chef of restaurants Aquavit and Riingo, and a connoisseur and maker of fine food, Marcus is at the same time very real and down to earth. He is uniquely aware that food is much more than just something good to eat. As he says in the series, "Everywhere I've been, everything I am, is reflected in my feelings about food."

I'm hoping that *The Meaning of Food*—which crisscrossed the United States gathering food stories from a wide variety of people and cultures—will help shed some light on who we are as Americans. You'll find the stories in this book, and in the PBS series (available on DVD through PBS Home Video), along with an accompanying Web site on pbs.org.

Dig in! Enjoy!

—SUE McLAUGHLIN

INTRODUCTION

The best meal we ever ate in New Mexico wasn't in any of the hip Nuevo Mexican restaurants of Santa Fe's central plaza or Canyon Road or even at the excellent Santa Fe Cooking School. Our best meal was nearly two decades ago in a little roadside restaurant at the edge of Española on the high road between Santa Fe and Taos.

We had spent the morning in the fields with chile pepper grower Orlando Casados as he showed us the peppers that his family had centuries ago carried with them from Mexico to the upper reaches of the Rio Grande. In the 1960s Orlando himself had brought them from the family's Spanish land-grant homestead in southern Colorado downriver to Española.

A stocky and handsome man, Orlando straddled a row and bent over to cup his hands beneath a pepper plant. Hidden from the hot sun by a thick tangle of leaves were tiny white flower buds. He smiled. He could not have been more proud of his own children.

And when the sun arched directly overhead, we all drove into town to his wife's restaurant, JoAnn's Ranch-O-Casados, for a feast in the guise of lunch.

We still had the soil of the fields on our shoes and the smell of raw green chiles on our hands when JoAnn sat us down in a back room off the kitchen and kept the dishes coming—dried corn stew called chicos, enchiladas blanketed with fresh green chile and brick-red adobo sauces, carne adovada as strident as a chorus of trumpets, chiles rellenos, bowls of thick menudo . . . and on and on until we finished up with hot sopapillas drizzled with local mesquite honey.

And that was just for lunch.

But we weren't eating lunch. We were eating history and culture. JoAnn had cooked the food that Orlando had grown from the seeds that his family had preserved, father to son, for centuries. Those plates represented the nexus of taste, identity, culture, and family. No wonder they were so good.

It is our great fortune to travel and write about it for a living. And while we don't always connect with people like Orlando and JoAnn Casados, we inevitably find that food is our doorway into the local culture, our point of entry to the local way of life.

When we arrive in a new location, we go first to the market. It's always an eye-opening—and mouth-

watering—experience. An elderly woman operating a slicer in the corner of the public market in Oporto, Portugal, revealed to us the secret for shredding Galician cabbage *just so* to make caldo verde. The lady who sold us her homemade cheese at an outdoor farmer's market at a mountaintop shrine in Spain's Sierra Aracena shyly introduced us to one of the goats she'd milked to make it.

We stood around the family patriarch on a reef island off Taha`a in French Polynesia as he showed us how to turn a fresh catch of reef trout into *poisson cru* with some chopped onion, lime juice, and fresh coconut milk. We helped build a fire for the underground oven so that when we all sat down to eat a few hours later, we could pretend to have done our bit to help our hosts.

To feed each other and to let ourselves be fed are among the most primal of human impulses and deeply satisfying of human pleasures. Food bridges gulfs between cultures, between people. Some travelers remember places best as a color, a look, the feel of the wind or the sea or the sun on their faces. We remember the smells and the tastes, the deli-cious contentment that comes from knowing through the senses. When we break bread together, we form a bond not easily dissolved. We remember and salute our *compañeros* of meals past—we will never forget you.

This book is meant to accompany the rich programs of *The Meaning of Food* created by Sue McLaughlin and her crew at Pie in the Sky Productions. The documentary and the book can stand alone, but we think that they go together like bread and wine, oil and vinegar, or sesame and rice. Neither, of course, can supply all the answers to that quintessential question *What is the meaning of food?* But we are pleased to present some context for considering the question.

We do suggest that *one* meaning of food is human continuity—even a kind of immortality of the species. Orlando Casados has passed away, but we still grow his chiles in the corner of our garden. As Marcus Samuelsson says in his toasts that end the documentary segments, "To life! To food! To us! Skoal!"

—PATRICIA HARRIS AND DAVID LYON

FOOD & LIFE

Taste lingers. It curls on the tongue with the sweet honey of memory, the bitterness of a broken promise, the salty heat of a midnight embrace. We never forget the tart rebuke of biting into an unripe fruit.

Flavor haunts us with the ripe pride of a cherry, the melting ooze of chocolate on the tongue, the soothing warmth of chicken soup, the earthiness of winter parsnips, the nutty tooth of barley, the snap of a chile pepper, the sheer milkiness of a glass of warm milk.

A piece of cake is never so simple as a piece of cake. It could mark the beginning of life or the end—or any one of the myriad messy points in between. Making a cake could be an act of grace and memory: Grandma's pound cake recipe served at her wake. A piece of cake might be as naive and direct as a child's birthday cake ablaze with candles of hope. Make a wish, we say. Or cake is the devil's food, a temptation to gluttonous lust. It translates as reward . . . or shame . . . or memories of home.

Food is the alpha and omega of human experience. It fuels our bodies and feeds our souls. As M. F. K. Fisher wrote in the foreword to *The Gastronomical Me*, "It seems to me that our three basic needs, for food and security and love, are so mixed and mingled and entwined that we cannot straightly think of one without the others. So it happens that when I write of hunger, I am really writing about love and the hunger for it . . . and then the warmth and richness and fine reality of hunger satisfied. . . . There is a communion of more than our bodies when bread is broken and wine drunk." When we break bread together, we are bound one to another—companion means literally "one who shares bread." Food means security. Food means family and friends. Food lets us express our pride, and it becomes a means to sustain and succor others. Food brings out our basest instincts and our higher natures.

In other words, food is the universal human experience. It figures in every human need, in every human motivation. But trying to answer the question *What is the meaning of food?* is as difficult as trying to answer its corollary, *What is the meaning of life?* In a very real sense, both physically and metaphysically, food *is* life.

WHAT IS FOOD?

We all know food when we see it—or think we do. The notion that "one man's meat is another man's poison" finds support in the Latin proverb *De gustibus non est disputandum*: "There's no accounting for taste."

Human beings are among the most omnivorous creatures on the planet; about the only things we cannot process are cellulose and certain other plant fibers. Under the right circumstances human beings will eat pretty much anything. And have. Worms, crickets, live eels, raw eggs, fermented cabbage, smoked fish, aged beef, black smut fungus—they're all on the human menu, and in some instances are considered delicacies. *De gustibus* indeed.

So what is food, after all?

At the biological level we eat not to feed ourselves as individuals, but to nourish the millions of cells that we carry around in the sack of seawater we call a body. We evolved from unicelled creatures awash in the ocean of nutrients, and our complex systems do their best to replicate

this condition on the cellular level, delivering simple sugar and oxygen to the cells and absorbing the waste carbon dioxide and water. Eons of evolutionary specialization have created an elaborate system for making sure each of us gets enough nutrition to keep our army of associated cells going long enough to reproduce.

Identifying food begins with taste, a phenomenon that is far more complicated than scientists once thought. Until quite recently conventional scientific wisdom decreed that all taste receptors were on the tongue, and that the tongue perceived only four sensations: salt, sour, sweet, and bitter.

Moreover, early taste researchers claimed, it was quite possible to map the tongue and show which parts were sensitive to which of these given qualities. Sweet was at the front, sour and salt on the sides, and bitter at the back as a final line of defense to keep us from swallowing some environmental poison that might do the body harm.

Common sense and millennia of experience tend to back up this simplification. We evolved the ability to taste sweet, the argument goes, so we can find high-calorie carbohydrates to eat. We sense salt so our food might replace the ions we've lost to sweat or excretion. Sour warns us of

ing glutamate and aspartate, and is found in high concentrations in soy sauce and aged cheeses.

Receptors for all five tastes are indeed located on the tongue's tiny onion-shaped taste buds. It has now become clear, however, that we sense each of the five primary tastes all over the tongue, though in differing degrees.

The mouth performs triage, but it's really the sensory systems in the nose that provide the information our brains translate as flavor. As the French gourmet and founding father of taste research, Jean-Anthelme Brillat-Savarin, wrote in 1825, "Smell and taste are in fact but a single sense, whose laboratory is the mouth and whose chimney is the nose."

Although philosophers, poets, and scientists since antiquity have postulated theories about the sense of smell, the biological mechanisms of smell remained elusive until the groundbreaking research of Richard Axel and Linda Buck. In 1991 they published a paper identifying approximately a thousand genes that code for specific smell sensors in the nose. Each sensor detects an individual chemical compound and relays that information to the brain. Indeed, so important is the sense of smell that 3 percent of human DNA is devoted to this single sense. Notably, Axel and Buck shared the 2004 Nobel Prize for Medicine

unripe fruit that might upset our digestive systems, and many truly bitter-tasting substances (strychnine, quinine, and cyanide salts, among others) can indeed be lethal.

The theories about *why* we taste sweet, sour, salt, and bitter haven't changed much, but the understanding of *how* we taste those sensations has, and the old taste map of the tongue has been largely debunked in the process. Moreover, cellular and molecular biologists have recognized a fifth taste called umami (named by Japanese researcher Kikunae Ikeda when he first identified it in 1909). Umami is the taste of certain amino acids, includ-

for their discovery and their continuing work in sensory neuroscience.

Taste ultimately lies in the brain, which processes signals from the mouth and nasal cavity and interprets them: *Aha!* says the brain. *A peach! And a ripe one at that!*

Fellow omnivores such as bears, pigs, and raccoons have similar taste systems. In fact, all mammals are similar on the biochemical level. But as Brillat-Savarin observed, "Animals feed while humans dine." Long before the biology of taste was understood, he also posited three different sensations. "Direct sensation" came from food when it first went into the mouth. "Complete sensation" resulted from chewing and swallowing, at which point sense of smell became involved. "Reflected sensation," he wrote, "is the judgment which conveys to the soul the impressions transmitted to it by the organ." Modern researchers might be more comfortable with the substitution of *mind* for *soul*, but his point is well taken. Taste, aftertaste, and remembered taste round out the sense.

WHAT IS A MEAL?

Perhaps the biggest leap from merely feeding to actually dining is the concept of a meal. Although archaeologists continue to debate the diets and culinary practices of prehistoric peoples, the earliest written records describe feasts that readily conform to the modern idea of a meal. Ethnologists argue that meals are constructed less of food, per se, than of juxtapositions and combinations of foods that carry their own layers of meaning. Protein connotes strength and status, starch comfort, sweet fruits and pungent vegetables excitement and variety.

As we generally recognize it, a meal mimics the dietary diversity of our species. It generally consists of a form of protein (fish, meat, eggs, tofu, dairy products, legumes, nuts), one or more fruits or vegetables, and a serving of starch. In *The Sun Also Rises*, Ernest Hemingway summed up the convention: "We had a good meal, a roast chicken, new green beans, mashed potatoes, a salad, and some apple-pie and cheese." Not all meals are so rounded. In a time of shortage, certain elements may be eliminated, but the dishes are prepared as if the protein-vegetable-starch triad were present— resulting in porridge from grains, a "mess of greens," or a thin broth of boiled bones. *Feasts*, on the other hand, are characterized by bounty: a cornucopia of vegetables, an array of pâtés and terrines, or the American buffet carving table laden with sliced ham, roast beef, leg of lamb, and turkey.

Yet for all its redolence and significance, the physical substance of a meal remains secondary.

A meal is not about food; it is about the human interchanges and interactions that go on around food. Rituals—both social and practical—transform mere food into a meal. To cook something, to serve it, to share it with others is a sequence fraught with meaning. "The other senses may be enjoyed in all their beauty when one is alone," wrote poet Diane Ackerman in A *Natural History of the Senses*, "but taste is largely social."

Her observation is an ancient one. Unlike every other species on the planet, humans do not eat simply when food is available. We dine at particular times, in particular ways, with particular tablemates. Plutarch distinguished civilized persons (Greeks and Romans, mainly) from beasts and barbarians (which he considered interchangeable) by their eating rituals. In his treatise on food in *Moralia*, Plutarch declared, "We do not sit at the table only to eat, but to eat together."

Plutarch could not have imagined some of our current dining arrangements. For its first three decades, the U.S. space program dispensed with tables aboard spacecraft, since engineers argued that they wasted space. But when American astronauts spent a long tour aboard the Soviet Mir space station, they reported that meals shared around a common table turned out to be a huge boost to morale. Based on that experience, Al

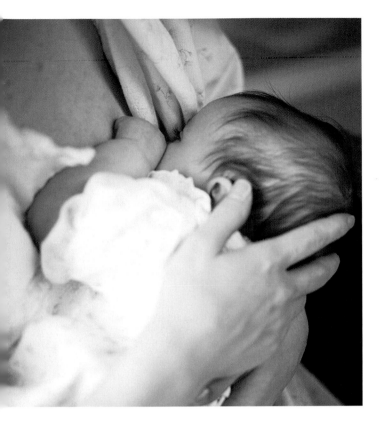

reaffirms not only our humanity but the joy of being alive." Human dining is meant to be a convivial social occasion. Food represents life in the joyous sense of good times, abundance, fertility, continuity, sensuality—of living to the fullest.

HOMEY FOOD

We are born hungry. Before we know anything of restaurants, or refrigerators, kitchens, cookies, or candy, we reach instinctively for the breast and we eat. Our first communication with another human being is also our first meal.

The taste of mother's milk binds us to the world. We are born belonging to our mothers and, by extension, to our mother's clan. In a broader sense we are also born to the flavors and food preferences of our mother's culture. The very chemicals that tickle her taste buds and set her olfactory sensors to quivering are concentrated in her breast milk. A mother who eats beans and tortillas and chile peppers passes on those same preferences to her suckling child. They become imprinted in our sensory memory bank. Garlic, mackerel, Gorgonzola cheese, the pungent durian

Holland, resident psychologist at NASA's Johnson Space Center, successfully argued for a dinner table aboard the International Space Station.

The social interaction over a meal is as substantive as the nutrition. As Marcus Samuelsson, chef and co-owner of Aquavit and executive chef of Riingo in New York, explains in *The Meaning of Food* documentary, "Through food, we express love. We bring comfort and hope. We forge new relationships, and reinforce old bonds. Food

Eating is more than a hand-to-mouth experience. The Japanese Restaurant Association estimates that, around the world, 1.5 billion people eat with knife, fork, and spoon; 1.2 billion eat with chopsticks; 350 million eat with knife and hands; and 250 million eat with hands only.

Oatmeal Raisin Cookies

Makes 2 dozen cookies

1¹/₂ cups flour
1 teaspoon baking soda
1 teaspoon cinnamon
1 cup butter at room temperature
1 cup brown sugar
¹/₂ cup granulated sugar
1 egg, beaten
1 teaspoon vanilla
1¹/₂ cups oats
1 cup raisins

Children love cookies. Chef Thomas Soukakos of Seattle makes this family-favorite recipe for his son, Alexander.

Preheat oven to 350 degrees. Sift flour, baking soda, and cinnamon into a bowl.

In a separate bowl cream the butter with the two sugars. Stir in the egg and the vanilla until combined, then add the oats and raisins. Add dry ingredients and mix well. Roll into balls and lightly flatten, then set 1 inch apart on baking sheet lined with parchment paper or Silpat.

Bake for approximately 20 minutes or until lightly browned.

fruit of Southeast Asia—we literally take them in with our mother's milk.

These tastes become the tastes of home and will remain powerful emotional triggers throughout our lives. Some psychologists call this phenomenon the Proust Syndrome, a reference to the stream of memory unleashed in *Remembrance of Things Past* when author Marcel Proust tasted a *petite madeleine* cake moistened in a little warm tea. The food of childhood is the food of home—not just "the place where they have to take you in," as poet Robert Frost once put it, but the place where the returning Prodigal Son is welcomed with a feast, even in a time of famine.

Developmental psychologists have long recorded that children from widely divergent cultures have remarkably consistent food preferences. Young children, in particular, tend to favor soft and moist foods over those that are crisp, dry, particularly spicy, or extremely hot or cold. (Ice cream is an exception to the "cold" rule, probably due to its sweetness.) They often like refined products—white bread over whole wheat, white rice over brown, and so on. But juvenile diets are usually just a subset of adult diets. While children may be less subject to social strictures on their eating than adults, few societies indulge their offspring by preparing separate meals for them once they have enough teeth to chow down on the family food.

The foods of home exert such a hold that people often carry their foodstuffs with them whenever they travel, like the New Mexican chile pepper farmer who took a supply of canned jalapeños with him on a Caribbean cruise. The alkaloid that makes chile peppers spicy-hot, capsaicin, also promotes the production of pleasure-inducing endorphins in the brain, a response that is heightened by repeated exposure. Chileheads get much the same high as runners get from vigorous exercise. Taste addiction aside, anecdotal evidence in the literature of psychology shows that many expatriates can alleviate depression only with the familiar foods of their upbringing. Culture shock is often culinary shock.

The urban community garden often holds culinary treasures that even the finest gourmet

Breast milk is brain food. British nutrition researchers compared the IQs of children who had been fed breast milk as infants with those of peers who had been fed formula. In a 1992 report in *The Lancet*, they concluded that breast-fed babies scored 8.3 points higher on a standardized IQ test, even after adjusting for the mother's educational, social, and economic status.

shops cannot replicate, thanks to seeds or cuttings brought from the Old Country. One such garden with fewer than two dozen plots in Cambridge, Massachusetts, blooms each summer with Puerto Rican sweet peppers essential for sofrito, hot peppers native to the Mexican state of Oaxaca and critical in preparing an authentic mole amarillo, the Jamaican braising green called calaloo, family heirloom okra from Mississippi, Indian ginger, and Andean amaranth. City officials threaten to take the land to build a handball court and a climbing wall; the immigrants shudder. What will they eat?

The impulse to eat *my own food* is so powerful that gastronomic imperialism has left as much of a mark on the world map as its military counterpart. In the West, the Greeks and Phoenicians began the process of spreading wine grapes, olive trees, and wheat to their Mediterranean, Near Eastern, and North African colonies. The Romans and their medieval successors, in turn, covered the Iberian peninsula with vines, trees, and grain, seeding Europe with the cornucopia of Latin cuisine—and inadvertently spreading citrus culture as well. Their Jewish gardeners took the sacramental citron tree with them wherever it would grow and brought the

Site of the U.S. record for jalapeño eating (141 jalapeños in fifteen minutes): Laredo, Texas

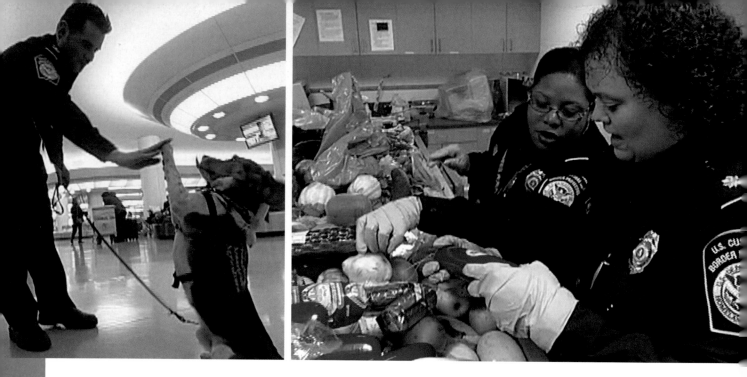

JFK AIRPORT CUSTOMS

The handout from the officers of the Animal and Plant Health Inspection Service (APHIS) is innocuous enough: "We regret that it is necessary to take agricultural items from your baggage. They cannot be brought into the United States because they may carry animal and plant pests and diseases. Restricted items include meats, fruits, vegetables, plants, soil, and products made from animal or plant materials. . . ."

APHIS officers pass out a lot of these notices every day at New York's JFK International Airport, but the blandly bureaucratic wording does little to placate travelers who have packed their baggage with their particular versions of comfort food.

"Sometimes there's more food in their bags than clothing," one officer at Customs explains. Another pipes in, "We've opened up suitcases and found a whole leg—from pork that somebody had turned into a ham. One day we got two frozen calf heads in a bag." Yet another officer notes, "These

are things that they may not be able to purchase in our country."

More than 250,000 people a day enter the United States, and a surprising number try to bring the tastes of home with them. "Some of them will tell you that the food over there tastes better than food over in the United States," adds an officer with obvious sympathy.

But food smugglers are likely to meet up with a canine from the APHIS Beagle Brigade, dogs chosen for their acute sense of smell and gentle demeanor with strangers.

As a perky beagle named Banjo darts from bag to bag, sniffing assiduously, customs inspector Joseph Demalderis explains, "The dogs all differ in their responses to the luggage. Some of them'll go really crazy on meat. They'll get excited, and when they hit on a plant material, it's basically they just walk up and sit down, which is supposed to be their response."

If the meats, fresh fruits, or vegetables are on the contraband list—and most meats and fresh

fruits and vegetables are—they will be seized. The law permits APHIS to punish travelers carrying undeclared food with fines of up to $50,000, though they are rarely imposed.

Half of the contraband room at JFK looks like a gourmet butcher shop, with its mounds of twisted sausages, shrink-wrapped hocks, and whole air-cured and vacuum-packed pieces of serrano and prosciutto ham. (The two million interceptions of illegal agricultural products each year include almost 300,000 lots of meat and meat by-products.) The produce section might be the world's best fresh market, piled high with exotic fruits and vegetables that include jackfruit from Bangladesh, fresh olives from Greece, moringa pods (called "drumsticks") from Guyana, ripe chiles from Mexico . . .

Travelers often don't give up their groceries without at least a plea. Every agent has a story.

"People in essence don't know what they are bringing. They just know that they are bringing 'the fruit from my grandmother's garden,' " one says. Another nods: "That could be Grandpa's famous recipe for salami."

A female agent affects a singsong voice, mimicking a hypothetical smuggler as she holds a golden apple with a rosy blush. "'This is from the sacred tree. The sacred tree! You must let me pass with this. It was passed down through many generations.' "

Inside the contraband room, the illicit goods—the tastes of home—swirl down the drain of a giant garbage disposal.

ABOVE FROM LEFT TO RIGHT: Customs inspector Dan Huss and Banjo. Inspectors Rena Cruz and Gina Reneau in the contraband room. Agent James Armstrong surveys a portion of one day's intercepted produce.

closely related lemons and oranges. While citrus culture suffered in the centuries after the fall of the Roman Empire, North African Arabs reintroduced the lemon and orange through al-Andalus, later known as Spain.

Not everyone complained. Indeed, sometimes the omnivorous human will embrace new tastes. Imagine Neapolitan food without tomatoes and peppers from the New World, or Irish cuisine without the South American potato. In reciprocal fashion, the conquistadores brought pigs, cattle, and chickens to the New World—and took home turkeys, maize, pumpkins, and the line of beans that would eventually become the French *haricots verts*. The missionaries who followed only steps behind the soldiers brought wine grapes to the New World so they could continue to produce sacramental wine.

The dispersion of foodstuffs to alien shores has not yet slowed. In the nineteenth and twentieth centuries, canned corned beef and, later, Spam became ensconced in the diets of Pacific Islanders. (Travel essayist Paul Theroux noted during his journeys among these islands that wherever the

State with the most Spam consumption at an average of 5.5 cans per person per year: Hawai`i

people had once practiced cannibalism, they now ate Spam.) And while some Frenchmen may weep at the sight of golden arches on the Champs-Élysées, the quintessentially American hamburger has taken France by storm.

In a 1985 exhibition celebrating national characteristics in consumer design, London's V&A South Kensington Museum, then the Victoria & Albert, selected a single object to stand in for the whole of each national culture. For the United States of America, the icon was the hamburger: "Mass-produced, cheap, efficient, but essentially juvenile," the curators noted in the exhibit label. (Americans need not feel demeaned. The museum elected to sum up the United Kingdom with a commode.)

SACRAMENTAL FOOD

So-called primitive societies often use elaborate food rituals, including hunts, feasts, and food exchanges, to mark the transition from childhood to adolescence. American culture tends to downplay the role of food in the dawn of sexuality, but families with deep religious roots still feast when a child has a bar or bat mizvah, is confirmed into the church, or is baptized into the adult congregation. It is a cause for celebration, and food is inevitably part of that celebration. At the same

BURGER CULTURE

- Site of world's first hamburger chain: White Castle (est. 1921), Wichita, Kansas
- Record holder for world's largest hamburger (3,591 lb): Rutland, North Dakota
- City with oldest operating McDonald's (est. 1953): Downey, California
- Places claiming to have invented the hamburger:
  New Haven, Connecticut
  St. Louis, Missouri
  Hamburg, New York
  Seymour, Wisconsin
  Summit County, Ohio
  Athens, Texas

time the child joins the adults at the table—a transition that in more secular families may be marked by a seat at the grown-up table during holiday gatherings—he or she is expected to assume adult responsibilities, such as fasting at Ramadan or during Lent, or observing taboos on the consumption of certain foods. In hunter-gatherer societies the passage out of childhood signals taking on adult tasks such as gathering and preparing food. In America it may mean loading the dishwasher after dinner.

Few life changes are as sweeping, however, as marriage, when children (at least in theory) leave the homes of their parents to establish families of their own. Every culture has food rituals integrally linked to this life passage. In the Trobriand Islands of Papua New Guinea, for example, the kin of the man and woman have traditionally engaged in an eight-stage process of exchanging food. (The elaborate ritual was first described by anthropologist Bronislaw Malinowski in *The Sexual Life of Savages in North-Western Melanesia* and subsequently confirmed by succeeding generations of social scientists, who have flocked to Papua New Guinea the way aspiring chefs pay their dues in the restaurants of Paris.) The pre-matrimonial transfer of larders begins with an offering by the woman's family members to acknowledge their assent to the union. Three rounds of reciprocating food gifts between the families follow, until the man's father finally makes a large gift of food to the woman's father. Then and only then can the wedding take place—possibly because both families have accumulated

FLAVORS OF HOME

It's not always necessary to smuggle in flavors from the Old Country. In Chicago, Richard Zhiri serves food that transports his fellow Africans back home.

Richard bustles back and forth between the kitchens of TBS African Restaurant and his insulated delivery truck. "I sell a hundred meals on the average day," he says, displaying each pot as he loads it. "I have the plain white rice, the jollof rice, goat, beef, tripe, cowskin. . . ."

Richard takes the wheel and heads for an area near Chicago's downtown where the city's taxi drivers congregate. "My typical customer is the African cabdriver," he explains. "The Nigerian cabdriver is the majority." Most of the drivers work shifts of twelve to eighteen hours. Richard's truck is an oasis of home on the streets.

"I'm having what they call pounded yam," says one driver as he digs into a plate of mashed vegetable. "This is a Nigerian food."

The cabbies descend on Richard, hungry for African food. "We like our food to be oily, with red oil, and to be hot. Pepper!" says another driver between mouthfuls.

A broadly smiling cabbie leans out his window to show off his meal. "I got tripe. I got fish. This is plaintain and beans, which is four dollars. You can't beat that." He takes a bite and muses, "Any day I work, I'm always here. It represents the traditional food of Africa, which is more like unique, and more like you're back home. You can get what you want."

Richard nods. "Maybe that's the way they keep in touch with home, through their mouths," he says.

TOP LEFT: Richard Zhiri serves lunch. BELOW: Cabdriver Julius Osunde tucks into his hot lunch. RIGHT: Victoria Oniamusi prepares food at TBS African Restaurant.

Pounded Yam (Fufu)

Serves 2

2 cups water

2 cups yam powder

Every day, Richard Zhiri loads his insulated delivery truck with hot, tasty African food from TBS African Restaurant in Chicago. His customers flock to his truck for flavors of home, especially pounded yam or fufu. "Many Africans eat pounded yam every day and cannot consider life without it," says Richard. Fufu is a starchy paste, and the plant used to make fufu differs from region to region. Yam, cassava, plantain, sorghum, millet, rice, and corn are some of the plants that are dried and ground into a powder, but the preparation method is the same. The powder is cooked with water to make it stiff enough to roll into a ball. Use pieces of fufu to scoop up stew or sauce. Yam powder is sold at African food markets.

Bring the water to a boil in a 2-quart or larger pot. With the pot still on the stove, add the yam powder and mix well with a wooden spoon. The pounded yam is ready to eat when it smoothens and thickens into a dough. This process takes about 5 minutes.

Spinach Meat Stew

Serves 2

This hearty dish is another favorite of Richard Zhiri's customers. Although spinach is not indigenous to Africa, it was brought by colonizers. Africans also prepare this dish with pumpkin leaves. Jamaican red peppers can be purchased at African food markets.

Cut the boneless beef into small chunks and boil until tender. Drain well. Then deep-fry for 5 minutes. Remove from oil and drain on paper towels.

Cut the whiting into 6 pieces and deep-fry in the same oil for 10 minutes or until done. Remove from oil and drain on paper towels.

Blend the red bell pepper, Jamaica pepper, and tomato purees with the water. Put the mixture in a pot and boil over low to medium heat for 15 minutes, stirring every 3 minutes. Add the fried beef, chopped spinach, and 3 tablespoons of oil or peanut butter and boil for 3 more minutes. Add the fried fish and allow to stand for 3 minutes before serving. Serve alongside fufu or rice.

1 pound boneless beef

1 whole whiting fish, deboned

1 red bell pepper, pureed

1 or more Jamaican red peppers, pureed, or substitute any chile peppers

1 ripe tomato, pureed

1/2 cup water

1 1/2 cups vegetable oil (for deep-frying)

3 tablespoons vegetable oil, or substitute 3 tablespoons peanut butter

1 10-ounce package chopped spinach

enough food to put on a feast for the village.

The concept of the marriage feast is ancient. Four thousand years ago, Mesopotamian stone tablets tell us, a wedding was concluded by anointing the head of a bride with oil and organizing a banquet in her honor. Two millennia later the formula had only been elaborated, as Christians might recall from John's story of the marriage at Cana in which Jesus was said to turn water to wine so that the feast might continue. In the sixteenth century rustic Britons celebrated weddings not with wine but with their indigenous intoxicant, ale. A family would brew a large batch of ale from malted barley to slake the thirst of their guests at a daughter's wedding. The feast itself was called the bride ale—the origin of the modern *bridal*.

EROTIC FOOD

The historic rationale behind marriage was procreation—the injunction in the book of Genesis to "be fruitful and multiply." In ancient Rome wedding cake wasn't eaten; it was thrown at the bride, because the Romans believed that its main ingredients, wheat and barley, were powerful symbols of fertility. The shoes dangling behind the automobile grease-painted JUST MARRIED represent the vestiges of the European custom of putting a piece of bread in the bride's shoe to guarantee fertility. The casting of grain—in the American custom, rice or its ersatz surrogate, confetti—at a newly married couple has the same origin.

The association of grain with fertility seems only natural in agrarian societies, where a handful of seeds in a good growing season can be almost magically transformed into bushels of food. Indeed, fertility practices across the globe often involve small edibles that multiply. In parts of rural China, newlyweds find their matrimonial bed strewn with candied lotus seeds—lotus being another extremely prolific seed producer. Lotus seeds are also cooked with red beans for a soup served at the wedding banquet. The dish symbolizes the traditional hope that the newlyweds will be blessed with a child each year, a fecundity on which the current Chinese government profoundly frowns. The same soup often shows up at the New Year's table to ensure prosperity for the coming year.

Eating and sex are our strongest physical urges, basic to survival. But the connection goes much deeper. The joys and pleasures of food and mating are in some ways the very definition of being alive: a celebration of creation. Human culture often blurs the line between the two—and so does

LOVE ITALIAN-AMERICAN-STYLE

"This weekend is special. My daughter is getting married," proclaims Mike Piancone as he sits in his Italian gourmet shop surrounded by jars of pickled peppers, trays of paper-thin prosciutto slices, and shelves loaded with gallon tins of his proprietary olive oil. "I promised to do a real Italian feast."

Even as Mike contemplates the task of preparing a wedding dinner for twenty tables of guests at the family's suburban San Diego villa, cake maker Iren Gerzsenyi is in the Piancone kitchen piping large violet roses onto twenty-one separate wedding cakes, one for each table and one for the bride and groom.

"It was my mom's idea," explains bride-to-be Michele. "Since we're doing everything family-style, we thought that would fit in perfectly."

Since time immemorial, people around the world have marked matrimony with a feast that celebrates the future and honors the past. The pater familias, Piancone is going one step beyond tradition by preparing the food himself—his

blessing on his daughter's new life. True to their Italian heritage, their wedding reception will be marked by plates filled to overflowing. What greater blessing than abundance?

The day of the ceremony dawns clear and bright. In the early morning Piancone chops mushrooms and spinach and rolls long tubes of veal braccioli in his pride and joy, his outdoor kitchen. He admits his secret fear. "I wake up in the morning sweating that I'll run out of food," he says. "That is my problem." Then he runs down a list of appetizers, some already prepared, others ready to go onto the grill or into the oven: arancini (cheese-filled rice balls), stuffed mushrooms, quail eggs, zucchini, loaves of crusty ciabatta . . .

. . . and chicken wings. Mike grins as he displays trays of the golden-brown finger food. "We got to be American."

Dressed to the nines and ready to walk his daughter down the aisle, Piancone expresses confidence. "Everything will be okay," he says. "We

have plenty of food, beautiful weather, and nice friends. That is all we need."

As the wedding concludes, the guests clap wildly when Michele and her new spouse, Gary Foley, linger over their first kiss as husband and wife. But Mike breaks the spell. *"Andiamo! Mangiare!"* he bellows—"Come on! Let's eat!"

Guests crowd around the outdoor tables to pile their plates high, stacking slabs of lasagna next to grilled Alaska salmon steaks crusted in rosemary and garlic. Champagne flows and laughter resounds. "What's the definition of an Italian wedding?" Mike asks rhetorically. "Lots of food, lots of fun, lots of love!"

Reflecting the sentiments of the happy crowd, one satiated diner pronounces the efforts a success on all counts. "They don't judge a wedding by what people eat," he says. "They judge it by what's left over. If there's not a lot left over, then there wasn't enough food."

The Piancones will be eating for days.

ABOVE FROM LEFT TO RIGHT: Wedding cakes prepared by Iren Gerzsenyi. Mozzarella, one of the meal's ingredients. Celebrants at the Piancone/Foley wedding. Mike Piancone prepares a wedding dish in his outdoor kitchen. BOTTOM RIGHT: Assorted pasta in the colors of the Italian flag.

Zucchini Salad

Serves 4 to 6

Mother-of-the-bride Lia Piancone shares one of her favorite family recipes. "My mother taught me this recipe when I was young," she says. "I like it because it is simple; I think all Italian recipes are simple."

Boil the zucchini cubes for 3 minutes in a small amount of water in a saucepan. Drain and cover with lemon juice, chopped garlic, and salt, and let marinate for 30 minutes. Drain off the excess lemon juice and add the olive oil. Mix the fresh mint into the salad. Chill until ready to serve.

3 zucchini, cut into cubes

2 lemons, squeezed

2 garlic cloves, chopped

Salt to taste

5 tablespoons extra-virgin olive oil

10 fresh mint leaves

biology. We have the same kind of touch sensors, called Krause's end-bulbs, on our lips, tongue, mouth, and sexual organs, and their neural pathways for stimulating the brain are very similar. Our mouths water when we catch the aroma of a favorite food—and when we're sexually aroused.

There may be other evolutionary reasons for the eroticization of food. Anthropologists argue that male and female proto-humans had two ways—sex and meals—to interact peacefully. Sharing meals can provide more common ground for couples than sex, since even the most ardent lovers eat more often than they copulate. So intimate is the connection that many cultures evolved taboos about men and women eating together in public. Yet sharing food has become central in modern Western courtship rituals—from the safe lunch date (so popular with dating services) to the seduction dinner. The American custom of new brides and grooms shoving wedding cake in each other's mouths is a public farce that mimics the private sensuality of hand-feeding a lover with sweets. The sheer sensuality of feasting has long been associated with sexual arousal, from the Roman orgy to the tavern scene in Henry Fielding's *Tom Jones*.

In *Like Water for Chocolate*, Laura Esquivel described the blending of libido and cuisine into the act of preparing food: "Not only Tita's blood but her whole being had dissolved into the rose sauce, into the quails, and into every aroma of the meal. That's how she invaded Pedro's body: voluptuously, ardently fragrant, and utterly sensual." In many cultures the word for "husband" translates literally as "the man I cook for." Among the Asante people of Ghana, it is assumed that a couple has a sexual relationship if the woman cooks for the man. The amount of "chop money" he gives her for food indicates how much he desires her.

We speak of having a "sexual appetite"; of being "hungry for love." Watch Emeril Lagasse demonstrate a recipe. Along with his trademark "*Bam!*" as he tosses a sausage into a pan of greens, he's as likely to lick his lips and ask rhetorically, "Can't you just feel the *love* in there?" On a coarser level, sexual slang is full of analogies to food, most of them best left to twelve-year-old boys. Men and women alike refer to an especially attractive member of the opposite sex as "a real dish" or as looking "good enough to eat." The Twi language of the Asante people uses the same verb—*di*—for "eating" and "copulating."

Folk wisdom suggests that particular foods either stimulate sexual arousal, increase fertility, or both. The Doctrine of Signatures—a type of sympathetic magic that says various plants can affect body parts they resemble—has a long

JAMAI SHASHTI

As Mita Guha prepares for the ritual feeding that will honor her new son-in-law, she has only one worry. "He doesn't eat seafood," she says. "But he's gonna try it."

Mita, who hails from Bengal in northern India, came to the United States as a young bride. Although her children are assimilated into American ways, she has also made sure that they honor their Bengali traditions, language, and food.

Now that daughter Roneeta has married Brooks Allen, Mita has gathered her family and friends for Jamai Shashti, a June ceremonial feast that links the jamai, son-in-law, with Shashti, the Bengali goddess of childbirth. For Brooks the ritual is even deeper than it would be for a Bengali son-in-law. By partaking of the highly traditional foods of Bengali, he is literally ingesting the culture.

"You pray to goddess Shashti to be blessed with children," says Mita. "That's why we treat our jamai so well, so that we can be blessed with grandchildren. That's the bottom line."

As the ceremony gets under way, Brooks sits cross-legged on the floor with Ashmit Bhattacharya, a son-in-law of Mita's extended family. Flowers and burning candles surround the two young men. The honored *jamais* are blessed with grass and puffed rice as family members blow conch shells and the women call out the shrill Bengali *ulu-ulu-ulu* incantation used on auspicious and ritual occasions.

After the blessing, Brooks and Ashmit sit side-by-side at a table covered with a white cloth. In the crowded kitchen the women scoop foods into small dishes to be served to the *jamais*.

"The best food that money can buy—we try to get it for them, the *jamais*," says Mita. Fish is highly prized in Bengal because it is associated with fertility (fish spawn in abundance) and wealth (the scales resemble coins). As a result, the menu includes three different fish dishes as well as prawns, chicken and mutton, dal (any of several dishes based on lentils, chickpeas, or other legumes), five different types of fried vegetables,

several sweets, ripe mangoes, and sweet yogurt.

As Brooks and Ashmit work their way through the array of dishes, the onlookers stand and nod their approval, waiting to see the sons-in-law try the delicacies before all the assembled family sits down to eat.

"The idea that the mother-in-law would like us to have children—that's a nice thing," says Roneeta. "And of course, we plan to have children, so I don't see anything wrong with it."

Thinking ahead, she continues, "I would really like my own children to be exposed to the Bengali culture as much as possible. I would like them to learn the language and to do things like Jamai Shashti where they understand and appreciate part of their heritage."

ABOVE FROM LEFT TO RIGHT: Mita Guha stirs a dish. Family friend Mitra Nag helps prepare the meal. Friend Sunita Saxena fries eggplant. Ashmit Bhattacharya and Brooks Allen wait for the ceremony to begin. BOTTOM RIGHT: Part of the menu includes fried lentils, sautéed spinach, french fries, vegetable chop, and fried eggplant.

history. King Louis XIV of France, for instance, ordered his gardeners to cultivate asparagus in hotbeds so that he could have a supply of the priapic vegetable throughout the year, not just in spring. Other foods alleged to increase potency or fertility have included shark's fin (shark's fin soup is still one of the most expensive items on Chinese restaurant menus), prunes (the Victorians gave them away free in brothels), camel's hump, and— of all things—green M&M's.

Perhaps the best-known aphrodisiac of modern dining is the oyster. EAT OYSTERS AND LOVE LONGER! proclaims a sign in the window of a seafood restaurant. There may even be a hint of truth to the thought—oysters are high in zinc, a mineral that plays a role in ovulation in women and testosterone production in men—but any effects are unlikely to follow immediately after a plate of oysters on the half shell.

Giacomo Casanova, the infamous eighteenth-century Italian libertine, swore by chocolate as an aphrodisiac when taken just before bedding one of his conquests. And in fact twentieth-century researchers have found that several substances in chocolate do affect the brain.

A lot of complicated things happen when you eat a bowl of Ben & Jerry's Chocolate Fudge Brownie ice cream. Chocolate contains about 300

known chemicals, including small amounts of the stimulants caffeine and theobromine. The stimulant effects, however, are minimal—comparable to decaffeinated coffee. Peter Barnham, a pharmacological researcher at Bristol University in Britain, suggests that the presence of the chemical phenylethylamine may explain most of the lift people get from eating chocolate. Known as the "love drug" because people who report being in love have high levels of it in their brains, phenylethylamine is closely related to amphetamines, producing a state of alertness and well-being by raising blood pressure and blood glucose levels. Researchers report that the substance reaches peak concentrations in the brain at the moment of orgasm.

But many foods, notably aged cheeses and red wine, contain much higher levels of phenylethylamine than chocolate does, so research has turned

to other fronts to try to explain why, "Of all foods, chocolate is certainly the most craved," as Peter Rogers of the Institute of Food Research in Norwich, England, puts it. In 1996 researchers from the Neurosciences Institute in San Diego published a paper in *Nature* that could explain chocolate cravings. They discovered that chocolate contains anandamide, a chemical that binds to the same receptors in the brain as the psychoactive ingredient in marijuana, THC. While anandamide is normally quickly metabolized in the body, Emmanuelle di Tomaso and his coworkers found that chocolate also contains two substances that block its breakdown and prolong its effects. Yet another chocolate chemical, theophylline, quickly relaxes smooth-muscle groups, including the bronchial tubes—it's sometimes used to treat asthma. Taken together in a cup of cocoa or a bonbon, theophylline and anandamide produce deeper breathing, increased blood circulation, increased sensitivity to touch, and a mild euphoria.

In other words, the biochemical evidence suggests that chocolate could be the ultimate comfort food.

FOOD DENIED

Chocolate is often the first food to disappear from the diets of Christians in the United States during the season of Lent, on the theory that to do penance, we should give up pleasure. But selective abstinence and its more drastic corollary, fasting, have religious roots that predate Christianity. Fasting is mentioned in the ancient Indian texts of the Mahabharat and the Upanishads, as well as in the Bible's Old Testament.

Not all faiths embrace voluntary food deprivation. In the traditional Hawaiian religious system,
each food represents a different deity, and the
believer is said to ingest the god or goddess's
mana by eating the food—hardly an invitation to
fasting. In premodern times Hawaiian rulers
were celebrated for their ability to eat up to six
times the amount of a normal meal.

But adherents of many other religions fast regularly. Devout Hindus and Jains abstain from all
food and water for a day and a half every fortnight
as a means of spiritual improvement. Observant
Jews fast on seven occasions each year, although
only two days are considered major fast days: Yom
Kippur, or the Day of Atonement, and Tishah-
b'Ab, which mourns several tragedies in Jewish history, including the destruction of the first and
second Jewish Temples and the expulsion from
Spain. Firstborn sons also fast before Passover as a
remembrance and thanks that the Jews were
spared when the Lord slew the eldest sons of Egypt.

The religious connotations of fasting carry
over into the secular and political world. As
Mahatma Gandhi demonstrated, a public fast can
be one of the most effective ways to imbue a cause
with moral authority. Gandhi's lesson was not lost
on other advocates; somewhere in the world on
any given day, someone is fasting for a cause.

Fasting is seen as a purification of the body through denial—a direct manifestation of the age-old opposition of flesh and spirit. Messianic religions, including Islam and Christianity, make fasting a central tenet. Islam calls upon adult believers to fast during daylight hours for the lunar month of Ramadan, traditionally the month in which the Holy Quran was revealed. The fast, called sawm, is one of the Five Pillars (duties) of Islam.

In the early days of Christianity, believers fasted to achieve spiritual purification as they awaited the imminent return of the Messiah. By the Middle Ages canon law regarding fasting came to emphasize its penitential aspect. Going without demonstrated the depth of an individual's repentance for past sins and was required during the Lenten season since, by doctrine, all Christians had the blood of Christ on their hands.

Protestant reformers famously rejected the Lenten fast. In 1522 several priests in Niederdorf, Switzerland, were discovered to be devouring sausages on Ash Wednesday in the company of their printer. (Swiss printers were apparently considered dangerous subversives at the time.) In what came to be known as "the affair of the sausages," the master of Grossmünster cathedral in Zurich, Ulrich Zwingli, decreed that Christians should have a free choice in the matter of fasting. To this day certain Protestant sects remain actively opposed to the practice, although some charismatic churches have turned to group fasts as a way to petition God for a favor. During the unusually fierce hurricane season of 2004, for example, a charismatic church in South Florida took credit for turning a storm away from their community through a congregationwide fast.

The practice of fasting has continued to evolve in the Roman Catholic Church as well. Prior to the Second Vatican Council in 1962, Roman Catholics refrained from eating meat or meat broth on Fridays—a practice defined by the church as abstinence. The church has since trimmed its sails: Catholics are now allowed one modest meal and two smaller ones on fast days.

SACRED FOOD

In her essay collection *Between Two Fires: Intimate Writing on Life, Love, Food & Flavor*, Mexican novelist Laura Esquivel observed that "There is not really much difference between talking about food and talking about religion. In most religions access to the divine occurs through the consumption of food—eating or drinking of, with, or for the

RAMADAN DIARY: GOING WITHOUT

Shatreen Masshoor is one of eight million Muslims living in North America. She's also a typical teenager who usually dresses for school in jeans and T-shirt. Instead of covering her long, dark hair, she pulls it away from her face in a knot. This is her senior year of high school. It's also the first year that she plans to fast for the entire month of Ramadan.

As Shatreen's mother, Rona, explains, "Ramadan is a very holy time. For Muslims, it is like our Christmas, the most important time of the year." It is a month of prayer and fasting capped with acts of self-sacrifice and charity. During this time Muslims do not eat or drink between sunrise and sunset. "Ramadan is about giving and sharing and thinking of others less fortunate than us."

When Shatreen's alarm clock goes off in the 4:00 A.M. darkness on the first day of Ramadan, she elects to sleep instead of partaking of imsak, the meal eaten before sunrise. By early afternoon she sits in her classroom so hungry, she finds it hard to concentrate. "I wish I'd eaten something

this morning before starting to fast. I'm starving."

It's a mistake she does not make again. As she joins her family in the kitchen for the predawn meal the next day, she asks, "Can I make it for a whole month? Can I make it even for a day? . . . Why am I doing this again?"

Midway through the fast, Shatreen observes, "Keeping the Ramadan fast reinforces my Muslim identity. Sometimes I feel kind of invisible. Ramadan isn't even on the American calendar. So I like to let people know who I am."

She also acknowledges an unexpected bonus: "My family cooks better during Ramadan." She grins. "All my Muslim friends say the same thing."

During the last week of the fast, Shatreen joins her mother in the kitchen as she prepares the iftar—the evening meal, served after sunset. Her mother sautés lamb with onion, then adds tomato, salt, black pepper, and a little water. It will cook in a pressure cooker for fifteen minutes. Then they make goshfiel, a typical Afghan dessert of fried

dough sprinkled with powdered sugar. "It's just really good and really crunchy," Shatreen explains.

As the month draws to a close, Shatreen has had time to reflect on the benefits of this test of willpower. "Ramadan does give you a sense of completion," she says. "And I love to sit with my mother and share those first dates before we begin the real meal."

A phone call to her grandfather reveals why dates are traditionally the first food eaten to break the fast. "The reason is because Arabs had a lot of dates," Shatreen relays, covering the phone and calling out to her mother. "For them dates are the fruit of heaven." The Masshoors are Afghanis, not Arabs, but they follow the traditions of Islam.

On Eid, the last day of Ramadan, Shatreen goes through her routine at school but thinks about the importance of the evening to come. "It's strange being in school on such an important holiday," she says. "I have only a few hours to go. Every day I fasted it got a little bit easier and I felt a little bit stronger."

Finally Shatreen and her family exchange gifts as they embrace in the living room. "The next few days will be like Christmas, only better," she says. "We'll all get gifts. We'll be with family and we'll eat great food—even before the sun goes down. It's interesting how food tastes so much better when you break your fast on time, as opposed to when you cheat." She pauses. "I've not been cheating, of course. I made it. Thank God."

ABOVE FROM LEFT TO RIGHT: Rona Masshoor models a goshfiel, or pastry elephant's ear. Rona and daughter Shatreen take imsak, the meal before sunrise. Goshfiel, an Afghan dessert. Rona and family celebrate Eid, the culmination of Ramadan.

Chicken or Lamb Pelau

Serves 6

"My family cooks better during Ramadan," says Shatreen Masshoor. One of the Afghani dishes her mom, Rona Masshoor, prepares for iftar—the meal after sunset that breaks the daily fast—is pelau. It can be made with chicken or lamb.

Wash the rice three times, changing the water each time. Soak rice for a half hour to one hour.

Meanwhile, heat oil in large pan or pot over medium heat. Add onions and brown lightly. Add tomato paste, salt, pepper, coriander, and garlic. Sauté for 2 minutes. Add chicken or lamb and water and simmer meat until tender—a half hour for chicken, an hour for lamb.

Preheat oven to 450 degrees.

While meat is simmering, boil several quarts of water in a dutch oven or other large, lidded pot. Add rice and boil for 4 to 5 minutes until softened but still firm, like al dente pasta. Strain water from rice and return rice to the pot.

Add cardamom and garam masala to the rice.

Make a depression in center of rice and, with a slotted spoon, put the meat in the depression. Cover the meat with the rice that surrounds it, then cover rice with sauce.

Using the handle of a wooden spoon or a chopstick, poke five holes through the rice and meat mound to allow steam to escape. Cover pot and put it in the preheated oven for 10 minutes. Reduce oven temperature to 350 degrees and continue cooking for another 20 minutes.

Serve on a large platter. Put the meat in the center of the dish and surround it with a ring of rice.

4 cups basmati rice

3 tablespoons vegetable oil

2 large onions, chopped

2 tablespoons tomato paste

1 tablespoon salt

Black pepper to taste

1/2 teaspoon ground coriander

3 large cloves garlic, finely chopped

3 cups water

1 chicken, cut into pieces, or 5 pounds lamb shanks

1/2 teaspoon cardamom

1/2 teaspoon garam masala

deity is a common basic ritual. The profound significance of food in our daily lives has a great deal to do with our thirst for eternal life."

The Hindu festival of Annakuta, "the Mountain of Food," makes the connection explicit with spectacular ritual offerings of prasadam, literally "God's leftovers." Prasadam is the spiritual food of Hindus, first offered to the gods and then consumed by the devout. Each bite is a divine communion. Over several days an elaborate, wholly vegetarian feast is prepared and arrayed in the temple. Pilgrims arrive on the festival day to witness the offerings to Lord Krishna. When the ceremony is over, the food becomes God's leftovers, a substance so holy that it can be eaten off the floor without fear of contamination. So powerful are these leftovers that a fly partaking of a morsel will advance many lives in its next incarnation.

The impulse to consecrate food is as old as human religion. The modern practice of saying grace is a vestigial form of the more profound ritual of sacrifice—from the Latin *sacrificium*, "to make holy."

Few modern Americans have a direct personal connection to their food sources. They do not raise crops or tend livestock. Some hunt or fish for sport, but few do either for sustenance. Food comes from a grocery store, a bakery, or, in the extreme, a garden plot or a farm stand. The ancient practice of religious sacrifice, although still a part of the rituals we inherited from agrarian or pastoral ancestors, thus lacks the sting that our forebears felt. For a shepherd to slaughter one of his lambs diminishes his flock. In less affluent cultures than ours, such sacrifice might even seem counterintuitive. Those giving up their sustenance, however, assume they will be rewarded by improved relations with the spirit world.

In *Work and Days* the poet Hesiod explained the classical Greek practice of offering a blood sacrifice before every important meal as penalty for humankind's fall from grace with the gods. In the beginning of the world, he wrote, "meals were shared, and humans and immortals sat together." But when Prometheus stole fire, Zeus was enraged and banished humans from the

Botanists have identified more than 75,000 edible species of plants, and humans have eaten about 7,000 of them over the span of history. Yet the modern world depends on only about 20 species (mostly grains) to provide 80 percent of the world's food.

Olympian table. Ever after, said Hesiod, humans offered sacrifices before each feast as a symbolic entreaty to the gods to join them on earth.

Animal sacrifice predates the Greeks, although it is unclear from the archaeological record whether early sacrificial practices were limited to animals. Bones have a way of surviving better than vegetables or grain, and ancient records may have mentioned animal sacrifice most prominently because slaughtering an animal entailed a greater loss than the sacrifice of vegetable or grain.

The book of Genesis is filled with references to sacrifice, most poignantly Abraham's trembling willingness to sacrifice his only son (Isaac in the Judeo-Christian tradition, Ishmael per the Quran) until God delivers him a ram to use in the boy's place. Genesis is explicit that the ram was a *burnt* offering—that is, the animal was roasted and presumably devoured—and theologians and anthropologists alike mark the story as a watershed between human and animal sacrifice in Western cultures. The book of Kings relates what must have been one of the greatest animal sacrifices of antiquity. When Solomon's Temple was dedicated (circa 963 B.C.), the king sacrificed 22,000 cattle and 120,000 sheep. In keeping with Hebraic tradition, the carcasses were no doubt roasted and distributed to the populace.

On a less grandiose scale, religious sacrifice of livestock plays a role in ensuring equal distribu-

tion of food in smaller communities. Writing in the mid-twentieth century, British anthropologist Edward E. Evans-Pritchard described the calculations of the Nuer people, a cattle culture of southern Sudan, in their ritual sacrifices. Their traditions required the sacrifice of a cow or calf for important family celebrations, such as a wedding, or to appease the gods in time of drought or sickness. The meat from the sacrifice was parceled out to the entire community. Family obligations rotated to guarantee a steady supply of protein to all, for the Nuer would not even think of slaughtering an animal simply to provide food. If a given family had been hard hit with sacrificial duties, then it could elect to substitute a sheep or goat—even a wild cucumber!

From its earliest days Christianity, which arose as a religion of the urban poor, substituted the sacrifice of bread for the sacrifice of flesh—a reflection both of the lower socioeconomic status of Christians in the ancient world and of an ascetic distancing from animal nature. In the Catholic Mass the wafer is imbued with the attributes of flesh, echoing the New Testament words of Jesus, "This is my body." The community of believers is then welcomed to partake of the bread in emulation of the Last Supper. Interestingly, Spanish chroniclers of Mexican cultures at the time of European contact found a similar practice involving corn in the rites of Kukulkán, the Mayan analog to the Aztec god Quetzalcoatl. (The Aztec deity demanded human sacrifice; the

LAST MEAL

Few of us make deliberate decisions about our last meal—or even know which meal will be the final one. But the men and women who have faced the ultimate punishment of the justice system chose their final dinners before going to their deaths. Perhaps no one knows those choices better than Brian Price. While serving eleven and a half years in a Huntsville, Texas, prison, he prepared the last meals for more than 200 men and women who had been condemned to die.

Now a free man, Price recalls how he was drawn into the duty as he labors over the stove in his Crockett, Texas, home. A musician and professional photographer before he ran afoul of the law, Price was randomly assigned as a cook. When his turn came up to prepare a last meal, he resisted. "Most guys didn't want to be the last meal chef because it's a dark and morbid thing," he says quietly. "It gave them the creeps."

Yet when the man for whom he had cooked sent word back to thank him, Price shouldered the burden. "I told the captain, 'I'll do the last meals from now on. You don't have to worry about assigning them to anybody.' "

The condemned's wish was not always honored to the letter, as the prison did not have the resources to purchase exotic foods. So Price labored to do the best he could with what he had available. "If someone was to order shrimp or lobster, they would get a piece of frozen breaded fish . . . ," he says, his voice trailing off. "I would wash the breading off of it, and I would cut it diagonally so it would look like little triangles. And I had my own batter that I would dip it in and fry it in. It came out pretty good."

The labor became a way to bring dignity to an ignominious death. Price, who now operates a radio ministry with his wife, Nita, came to understand the power of a simple meal to provide succor when mere sustenance no longer mattered. "What if that was your son or your brother?" he asks. "Would you be so ready to see him put to death like a dog? Or would you rather see him get a good last meal?"

Price was especially taken aback when inmate Tom Gentry requested a bowl of butter beans before his execution. "He could have a steak, he could have just about anything he wanted. Why butter beans?"

As Price meditated on Gentry's unusual request, he recognized the solace many people find in the familiar, particularly in familiar food from childhood. "It must've been something he had when he was a kid," Price reflects now. "And I thought, *Maybe this little bit of food will give him some comfort, and take him back home when his mom used to cook him these things.*"

As the chef to the condemned, Price says, his aim was simple. "I'd pray that the meal would be enjoyed, if you would, and it would give them a little bit of peace."

ABOVE: Brian Price and his wife, Nita Baker Price, cook at home.

Mayan version was satisfied with corn. The Mayans considered the Aztecs barbarians, while the Aztecs dismissed the Mayans as effete.)

Ritual slaughter of livestock is relatively uncommon in American culture. One exception is the Afro-Caribbean religion Santeria, in which animals are sacrificed for divination rather than mediation between physical and spiritual realms. Imagine the outcry if we had televised slaughter of livestock as part of the swearing-in ceremony for a new president! Yet widely celebrated holidays still echo the age of sacrifice, as in the traditional vernal equinox meal (Easter or Passover in Judeo-Christian tradition) of spring lamb or kid.

HOPEFUL FOOD

Every *please* requires a *thank you*. The concept of thanksgiving—which survives largely in American religious culture in the form of prayer and in the secular culture as an overabundant meal starring roast turkey—represents one of the oldest of human impulses: gratitude for being blessed with the sustenance to survive. In hunting societies the conclusion of a successful foray is almost always celebrated by a burnt offering of some part of the kill (frequently the heart). Pastoral cultures follow the spring birthing with the sacrifice of a newly weaned animal. Agricultural societies tend to focus on the harvest. In Ghana the yam harvest sets off a three-day festival of Homowo that begins with blessings of the yams and of twins and triplets born during the year, and concludes with a massive feast. Traditionally, both the Irish and the Scots have celebrated Lammas at the end of the wheat harvest. The name translates from the Gaelic as "loaf mass." A loaf made from the first cutting of the wheat is taken to church, where it becomes the bread of the Eucharist. At some level, humans have always felt the need to tithe to the unseen world.

Although the American holiday of Thanksgiving is often associated with the Pilgrims of Plymouth, Massachusetts, their first Thanksgiving was in fact a spring worship service in 1621 to give thanks that 51 of their original 102 settlers had survived the winter. Not until the fall of 1621 did they celebrate an English-style Harvest Home feast with the Wampanoags, and in keeping with the Pilgrims' strict Calvinism, that observance had no overt physical sacrifice associated with it. (That would have been a Papist thing to do.) Not until Abraham Lincoln first proclaimed Thanksgiving as a national holiday in 1863 did the autumn celebration assume the overtones of sacrifice—not of food but of soldiers slain on the field of battle.

After the Civil War, Thanksgiving quickly reverted to its ancient roots as a fall harvest festival, yet the symbolic offerings to a deity have remained, if in somewhat muted form. The Congregational church that is the successor congregation to the Plymouth Pilgrims, the Church of the Pilgrimage, marks the Thanksgiving holiday with an altar laden with the fruits of the harvest and the symbolic cornucopia (a pagan symbol of plenty) made of bread.

Just 30 miles away the fishermen of New Bedford, Massachusetts, regularly land the most valuable annual catch of any port in the United States. Accordingly, each Thanksgiving season the Seamen's Bethel, a nondenominational Protestant chapel for seafarers operated since 1832, marks a Thanksgiving of the Harvest of the Sea with prayers of thanks—and an altar covered with fresh seafood.

Loaves and fishes—these simple foods have a deep resonance for Christians, recalling the New Testament story of Jesus preaching to a large and hungry crowd. His disciples could find only five loaves of bread and two fishes to feed the multitude. He blessed them and instructed the disciples to distribute the food to the crowd. When all were satisfied, twelve baskets of food remained.

RECIPES OF HOPE: IN MEMORY'S KITCHEN

Delicate as a bird, the older woman stands erect and proud behind a lectern as she speaks to an audience of teenagers and adults seated on folding chairs in a Long Island, New York, adult education class.

"My name is Bianca Steiner Brown," she enunciates very carefully with a Central European accent. "But for three years in Theresienstadt, or Terezín, I was only a number: the numbers BF621."

Bianca is a survivor of Terezín, which the Germans called Theresienstadt. During World War II approximately 144,000 Jews were transported to this Nazi concentration camp in Czechoslovakia about 40 miles northwest of Prague. In the 1990s Bianca completed an English translation of the book *In Memory's Kitchen: A Legacy from the Women of Terezín*, a collection of recipes originally handwritten in Czech and German on scraps of paper by the women in the camp.

"A lot of it took place in the evening when women could speak to each other, after lights went out," says Cara De Silva, the book's editor. "They would talk about who they were—who they had been—in terms of the foods that they cooked. They would exchange recipes. They would talk about foods, talk about their homes and the dinners they made. This was often called 'cooking with the mouth' because you had nothing to eat."

Bianca moved to the United States in 1951 and became a food editor for *Good Housekeeping* and *Gourmet*. She never met the woman who collected the recipes, Mina Pächter, an art historian. Mina was already in her seventies when she was incarcerated, and she became one of the 33,000 people who died

in Terezín even before the Nazis could send them to the death camps. But Bianca, who was about twenty when she was transported to Terezín, remembers well the conversations that took place at night.

"My bunk was the third one up and I tried to go to sleep and these women started discussing recipes," she says. "And I was so hungry. 'This recipe had four eggs . . . ,' and 'You have too much sugar . . . ,' or whatever it was. And I was so mad at them because I needed the sleep, especially since I had very little food, nourishment in me." She conjures up the specter of almost unimaginable deprivation. "Bread you got every two or three days. It was a quarter of a rye bread for those three days."

Cara, an editor, journalist, and former food and culture columnist for *Newsday/New York Newsday*, was surprised when she learned of the manuscript that Mina Pächter had entrusted to a friend before her death. After more than twenty-five years, the brittle pages finally found their way to Mina's daughter Anny Stern, who had fled to Palestine before the war and later moved to Manhattan.

"Initially the thought of women doing this was very shocking, because you just think of people who were starving to death as sort of resigning from the fleshly pleasures," Cara says. "And instead, what I discovered is that, on the contrary, I think it helped them to live, even though the food was imaginary. Because I think food nourishes not just the body, but the spirit."

Cara went on to discover fifteen other similar manuscripts, each poignant in its own way. She calls them "a real genre of Holocaust literature." In the

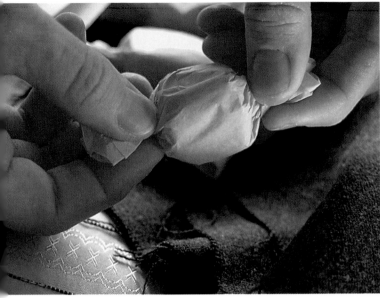

introduction to *In Memory's Kitchen*, she pointed out that "cooking, both doing it and talking about it, was central to the societies from which many of the women of Terezín, and most European women of the period, came. It was also among the chief activities that defined them as wives and mothers."

The Nazis sent many Czech, German, and Austrian intellectuals, prominent business people, and heroes of World War I to Terezín, which was initially maintained as a "show" camp to demonstrate to the world how well they were treating the Jews. The majority of the women who contributed to the cookbook that Mina Pächter compiled came from the Czechoslovakian middle or upper class, which had a sumptuous cuisine. "Robust, with sophisticated overtones, it was well known for its soups; its roast birds and smoked meats; its savory sausages and wild mushrooms; . . . its goulash and weiner schnitzel; its large variety of dumplings (eaten from soup to dessert); and its cheeses, such as hoop cheese (similar to a dry pot cheese); yeasted pastries

(part of a great baking tradition); palachinky, sweet crepelike pancakes; and, of course, beer," Cara wrote.

In Terezín the women remembered it all. They were the cooks who had prepared potatoes and herring, fashioned liver dumplings, stuffed a goose neck with farina, ladled goulash over egg noodles, rolled up a chicken galantine. Most of all they remembered the sweet breads and pastries that made them proudest: plum strudel, chocolate strudel, macaroons, linzer torte, apple dumplings, fruit bread, vanilla cake, gingerbread cookies. Memory was an act of love, and an act of defiance, as if the world they had known would someday return.

"There's a recipe in that book that I found for caramels from Baden," says Cara. "This woman would recite the ingredients. And then at the end, she said to wrap them in pink paper. And there was something about thinking about someone in a concentration camp carrying the fantasy of food that far—attempting to do it exactly right—that was such an incredible thought."

ABOVE FROM LEFT TO RIGHT: Wrapping caramels in pink paper. Bianca Steiner Brown.

In her bright modern kitchen, Bianca prepares a recipe from the book to share after her adult education lecture. Working with the steady purpose of an expert cook, she creams butter, adding sugar, ground hazelnuts, and grated lemon peel. She drizzles in a small amount of strong black coffee and spoons in melted chocolate, stirring well with her powerful mixer. Separately she beats egg whites until they are stiff and folds them into the butter-sugar mixture, alternating with a little flour. Each step is a ritual of remembrance. The Pächter Torte is Mina Pächter's legacy.

Bianca turns to a sheet cake, repeating the motions of another woman who had recounted her recipe as an act of defiance and a gesture of hope. When the cake is cool, she cuts neat squares, carefully arranges them on a platter, and dusts them with powdered sugar. Another cake, another woman's hospitality to guests.

After the adult education class, the cakes disappear swiftly as the students devour history and enter into a communion across the decades with the women of Terezín.

"Food is a powerful identity marker," says Cara. "It's one of the most powerful identity markers in the world—meaning the food of your childhood—what you grew up with, your celebrations, your memories of the meat loaf your mother made."

As the Nazis worked to obliterate the Jews of Europe, the women of Terezín "fought with Zwetschken cake [plum strudel] and Erdapfel Dalken [potato doughnuts] and things like that. In a funny way, it was fighting back when somebody's trying to erase you," Cara notes.

Her voice trembles with emotion. "I have come to feel that at some level it was being done for us. It was being done for the unseen others who might someday make these recipes again."

ABOVE: Bianca cooks Pächter Torte.

Caramels from Baden

In Terezín, a Nazi concentration camp in Czechoslovakia, women prisioners sustained themselves by exchanging their favorite recipes. This candy is one of those recipes, written in fragile handwriting on scraps of paper, that were collected by prisoner Mina Pächter and later published as the book *In Memory's Kitchen: A Legacy from the Women of Terezín*, translated by Bianca Steiner Brown and edited by Cara De Silva, and published by Jason Aronson, an imprint of Rowman and Littlefield Publishers, Inc.

Brown [caramelize] 30 decagrams sugar without water. Pour in 1/3 liter coffee extract [very strong coffee]. Add 1/8 liter cream and bring it to a boil. Add 8 decagrams tea butter [best quality butter] and cook until mixture is thick. Pour boiling into a buttered candy pan. With the back of a knife, divide it before it completely cools. Then break it into cubes and wrap in parchment and also pink paper.

U.S. EQUIVALENTS

8 decagrams = 2.82 ounces, or just over 1/3 cup

30 decagrams = 10.58 ounces, or almost 1 1/3 cups

1/8 liter = 4.25 ounces, or just over 1/2 cup

1/3 liter = 11.33 ounces, or between 1 1/3 and 1 1/2 cups

ETERNAL FOOD

If, as Laura Esquivel wrote, "we thirst for eternal life," then it could be said that death does not still our longings. While many cultures depict an afterlife of eternal feasting, many others seek to feed the wandering soul of the departed. Ancient Egyptians not only mummified the bodies of the deceased, but also provided favorite foods and beverages in the tomb to nourish them in the afterlife. The tomb walls of the wealthy were decorated with pictures of food, which would be magically transformed into sustenance should the need arise. Tombs of the ruling class also contained models of granaries, kitchens, and butcher shops—just in case the departed needed to go shopping. Egyptian families of less exalted rank made arrangements with the priests for periodic offerings of food to be made at the tombs of the deceased.

The custom of feeding the dead is observed casually in many places in the United States. It is not uncommon, for example, to find a shot glass and some nibbles left at one of the aboveground tombs in New Orleans. But few cultures can rival the Chinese when it comes to providing for the souls of the shadow world. The Festival of the Hungry Ghosts, which falls in the seventh lunar month of the Chinese calendar (usually in August), has its origins in placating the restless

spirits released from the underworld for a brief period each year. The spirits are hungry for the world they left behind, and are said to assume the forms of wild animals or even beautiful young lovers to seduce the living.

For up to two weeks, the community mounts public entertainment, such as classical Chinese opera performed in the streets, to distract the ghosts. Great tables laden with dishes of rice, chicken, bean curd, vegetables, fruits, and rice wine are set out nightly outside the gates of houses,

businesses, guild halls, temples, and associations to appease the restless spirits.

On the night before the full moon, families hold private indoor feasts to honor their ancestors with prayers and offerings on home altars. On the next night the feasting moves outdoors beneath the full moon, as the living eat and drink on behalf of the dead to send their sated spirits back to the underworld. In a public ceremony an altar is laden with sweet buns, candies, and cakes—which a priest blesses with great ceremony and then flings into the assembled crowd, scattering the spirits to whence they came.

The traditional Day of the Dead festivities of Mexico demonstrate a quite different attitude toward those who have passed to *el otro lado de este lado*—"the other side of this side," as poet and essayist Octavio Paz expressed it. The Day of the Dead is more joyous homecoming than fearsome haunting. In preparation, people decorate the family graves and set out small plates of food or bottles of beer for the departed.

A curious blending of pre-Hispanic Meso-american traditions and the feasts of All Saints and All Souls in the Roman Catholic liturgical calendar, El Día de los Muertos brings together the quick and the dead for merriment and feasting. Mesoamerican culture regarded death as just one more state of being in an endless cycle. The Mexican heirs to that culture may be as realistic and rational as any people on earth, but for a few days the fiesta allows them to "throw down our burdens of time and reason," as Paz wrote.

Families cover an altar with candles, photos or drawings of the dead, religious figures, bright ribbons—and food. Lots of food. An entire body of cuisine exists for the Day of the Dead. Sweet breads fragrant with anise and filled with dried and candied fruit and nuts are shaped to resemble a man, a woman, or a child. Some cooks bake rolls and embed tiny porcelain heads into them. No altar is complete without a quivering plate of flan.

The most labor-intensive and finest foods of the year are prepared for the Day of the Dead—rich tamales filled with stewed pork and chicken and wrapped in banana leaves, barbecued strips of beef smothered in a tangy tomatillo sauce, and the greatest seasonal dish of all, mole amarillo, or yellow mole. Its marigold-bright color is the traditional pigment of the dead, and marigold petals are used both in funerary practices and in Day of the Dead cooking. Small plates of all these delicacies are set upon the altar, while the larger communal bowls cover the family table and sideboards. American Thanksgiving has nothing on a traditional Day of the Dead meal. For one night each year, the entire family, living and dead, sits down to feast together.

From beginning to end, food is life.

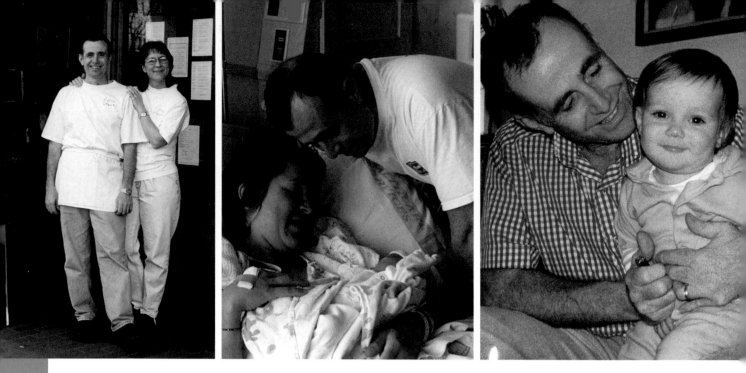

VIOS—A CELEBRATION OF LIFE

Thomas Soukakos is about to begin again. Shortly before the opening of his new restaurant, he sits in his Seattle living room surrounded by family photographs old and new and talks about food. "I grew up where food was like, great importance in our house," he recalls.

Born in Greece, Thomas came to live in the United States in 1985, bringing the memories and tastes of home with him. "When I was hanging out with my grandparents, all we talked about was food and wine, so it was really important for me growing up."

Food has also been at the center of his adult life. For nearly ten years he ran a popular restaurant called El Greco. It's where he met his wife, Carol—a trained chef, natural foods advocate, and dynamite baker—when she came to apply for a vacant position as a cook.

According to her close friend Richard Liedle, Carol shared Thomas's passion for food. "She once told me, 'I don't think romance is ever going to happen for me . . . and I'm fine with that. I'm going to make my food, and that's where my romance is,'" Richard recalls. "And in walks the Greek and turns her life upside down. It was the perfect union. It was the food meeting the soul for her."

Theirs was a marriage of a common fire, focused on a life together creating meals, sharing food, bringing a joie de vivre to family, friends, and customers. Five years after Thomas and Carol married, their son, Alexander, was born—just four days before the attacks of September 11, 2001. Richard remembers that he was still devastated by world events when he visited Carol after the birth of her son. "She put him in my arms," Richard recalls, "and she said, 'This is why we're going to keep living.' "

But it was not to be. Three weeks later, Carol descended into postpartum depression. Sadness spiraled into psychosis, and when Alexander was four and a half months old, she took her life. The family's world was turned upside down.

Thomas sold El Greco to concentrate on his new responsibilities as a single parent and to put

his life back together. Foremost on his mind was nurturing Alexander. "After I lost Carol, what I had left was my son, myself, and food," Thomas says.

But nearly three years later, Alexander was a lively toddler who sat on his father's shoulders as Thomas worked in the kitchen. The boy perched on the counter to stir a pan of green beans and even tentatively wielded a whisk to beat eggs.

It was clearly time for Thomas to open a new restaurant, where Alexander could grow up watching his father work and surrounded by an extended community of friends. "I feel like this is my obligation to my friends, community, neighborhood—to do what I can for them," Thomas explains. "To provide them with healthy food—a lot of depth, a lot of heart."

To celebrate the grand opening, the handsome red-walled room is filled with well-wishers—many children among them—who dance to the music of a balalaika and mill around platters of food. A framed photograph of Carol and Thomas has a place of honor, while big handwritten letters on a chalkboard proclaim CELEBRATE LIFE.

"I think Thomas is saying that our life continues even with this huge pain," says Richard, who has embraced his new role as Alexander's surrogate uncle. "We're going to remember Carol because she gave us this huge gift of Alexander."

Indeed, Thomas has named his new venture Vios—the Greek word for "life."

ABOVE FROM LEFT TO RIGHT: Thomas and Carol Soukakos. Carol and Thomas marvel over newborn Alexander. A moment of joy between father and son. Thomas and Alexander at dinner.

Carol's Famous Pear Almond Coffee Cake

CAKE

2 cups flour

1 teaspoon baking powder

1/4 teaspoon baking soda

1/4 teaspoon salt

1/2 teaspoon cardamom

1/2 cup butter at room temperature

3/4 cup sugar

2 eggs

1 teaspoon vanilla extract

1/2 teaspoon almond extract

1/2 cup sour cream

1 large pear, peeled and diced

TOPPING

2 tablespoons butter

2 tablespoons almond paste

1/2 cup brown sugar

1/2 cup chopped walnuts

1/4 teaspoon cardamom

Carol and Thomas Soukakos shared a passion for good food—and they loved to make treats for friends, family, and community. Carol was forever bringing people this pear almond coffee cake, her signature dessert.

Preheat oven to 375 degrees. Butter a 13-by-9-inch cake pan and set aside.

Sift together flour, baking powder, baking soda, salt, and cardamom. Set aside.

With a mixer, cream butter and sugar together until light and fluffy. Add eggs one at a time. Stir in vanilla and almond extracts. Fold the dry ingredients into the batter, alternating with sour cream. Gently add the pears. Spread batter in prepared pan.

Mix the topping ingredients together in a food processor or with a mixing spoon. Sprinkle over the cake batter.

Bake cake for 40 to 50 minutes in the preheated oven or until a tester comes out clean. Cool to room temperature before serving.

Chicken Sausage Pasta

Serves 4

Carol and Thomas Soukakos created this pasta preparation, which became a favorite in their restaurant, El Greco. "Everyone wanted Carol to make it for them, and I loved making it for her," Thomas recalls. At their restaurant it was often served as the nourishing dish of the day.

Roast the red bell peppers over an open gas flame until blistered, then place in an airtight container until cool. Peel, seed, and slice them.

Cook the chicken breast or chicken sausage in boiling water for 10 minutes. Drain and cut meat into chunks.

In a sauté pan over medium heat, warm some oil, and then add the slices of chicken sausage or chicken breast and cook until browned. Add shallots, garlic, and pepper flakes. Sauté gently until shallots and garlic are translucent, then add the sliced peppers and sauté until soft.

Deglaze pan with the wine, reduce completely, add the warm chicken stock, and let it further reduce until saucy. Add the tomatoes and basil near the end of the cooking and season with salt and pepper.

While the sauce is cooking, cook linguini in plenty of salted water until al dente. Drain. Add the linguini to the sauce and serve immediately in bowls, sprinkled with Parmesan cheese.

2 red bell peppers

Vegetable or olive oil

4 chicken sausages or 2 chicken breasts, cut into $1/2$-inch pieces

2 tablespoons shallots, finely diced

2 garlic gloves, chopped

Pinch of dried red pepper flakes

$1/4$ cup dry white wine

$1/2$ cup warm chicken stock

2 Italian plum tomatoes, seeded and chopped

Fresh basil, julienned

$1/2$ pound good-quality linguini

Freshly grated good-quality Parmesan

FOOD & CULTURE

Roughly 2,600 years ago in India, Vedic sage and healer Charaka observed, "You are what you eat," and people have been paraphrasing him ever since. It has become an article of faith that we are defined by what we eat, how we eat it, and with whom. The crudest slang reduces entire ethnic groups to a single dish from their cuisines, turning good food into bad feeling: bean-eater, cheese-head, white bread, chitlin, poi boy, meatball, kraut . . . Yet food speaks of a people's struggles and joys. It conveys a sense of place and circumstance, a body of shared history. And it is almost always the last vestige of ethnic identity surrendered as immigrants assimilate into main-stream America.

The Great Seal of the United States carries our national motto, *E Pluribus Unum*—Out of Many, One. In 1776 it reflected the unity of thirteen colonies. Over the centuries it has come to symbolize the rich diversity of the American people, drawn from hundreds of cultures around the world, yet banded together as a nation. The country used to be called a melting pot, but *stew* is perhaps more like it, with lots of individual flavors in the mix. Every successive wave of immigrants, as Marcus Samuelsson says, struggles "between holding on to our cultural heritage . . . and fitting in."

Our food is more than just something good to eat. It's an integral part of our identity. We are the bean-eaters, cheeseheads, white breads, chitlins, poi boys, meatballs, and krauts. And darn proud of it.

THE STAFFS OF LIFE

Perhaps borrowing from Charaka, French gastronome Jean-Anthelme Brillat-Savarin wrote in 1825, "Tell me what kind of food you eat, and I will tell you what kind of man you are." He could as well have written, "Tell me what kind of starch you eat, and I'll tell you where you came from." Bread and other staffs of life bind us together in unexpected ways, revealing our histories and our kinship.

In some parts of the world, the starch at the heart of every meal might be potatoes, manioc, or taro. But rice and wheat alone account for more than 40 percent of all the food eaten around the globe. Entire societies are built around these staple foods.

Every rice eater in the world owes a debt to Southeast Asia, the cradle of rice domestication, where cultivation began about 10,000 years ago. So central is rice to Asian cultural identity that it figures deeply in myth and legend. The folklore of the Kachin people of northern Myanmar relates that when the Kachins were sent from the center of the earth to populate the planet, they received rice seeds and directions to a place where the grain would flourish. Chinese myth, on the other hand,

Rice fields and paddies cover 11 percent of the earth's arable land and feed almost half its population. In many countries rice consumption accounts for more than two-thirds of daily calories and three-fifths of protein intake. Instead of greeting someone with "How are you?," Bangladeshis, Chinese, and Thais ask, "Have you eaten your rice today?"

claims that after a series of floods and famine, the people were rescued by a yellow dog that brought grains of rice on its tail. Tradition throughout China holds that "the precious things are not pearls and jade but the five grains." Rice, the staple of southern and coastal China, is first among them. Wheat, the staple of the north and the inland steppes, is second.

The rice world divides between two subspecies. People who eat one barely consider the other to be rice at all. The slender, long-grained indica rice unites cultures as far flung as southern India, the Middle East, West Africa, and the American South. It is a surprisingly short hop from the biryani of India to the pilafs of Lebanon and the hoppin' john of Alabama. Meanwhile the short-grained, chunkier japonica rice links the cuisines of China, Japan, and Korea with the tables of the Mediterranean. Risotto milanese is the distant cousin of the Chinese rice bowl. A preference for indica or japonica is a virtual litmus test of cultural identity.

The Breadboard

Humans were making a form of bread from wild wheat and barley kernels thousands of years before becoming sedentary farmers. Nomadic peoples gathered seeds of wild grasses, crushed them by rolling a round stone on a flat one, and added water to the coarse flour to make a paste. A kind of flat bread—so hard on the teeth that Neolithic skeletons show molars ground down to stumps—could be produced by grilling on a hot rock. It would have been something like uncooked pasta made with sand mixed into the dough. Somewhere along the way someone figured out that if you threshed grain onto a hot rock, it would become parched and would break more easily. Even more to the point, the parched, cracked grain could be quickly cooked into a kind of gruel that nourished many a nomad on the tribe's travels.

Geneticists pinpoint wheat's genesis in the Middle East—probably in the mountains of Israel and Jordan—from chance crosses of wild grasses. (The Israelites survived on cakes made from spelt, a primitive form of wheat, during the Exodus from Egypt.) Roughly 10,000 years ago humans began cultivating these hybrids, launching the domestication process that has led to "modern" wheat with its short stalks and easily removed bran.

The British Museum displays the world's stalest bread: loaves baked more than 5,000 years ago in Egypt. No one has pinpointed exactly when bakers started using yeast to make bread rise, though some wags have suggested that it was an accidental by-product of using yeast to make beer from sprouted barley. In the first century A.D., the historian Pliny the Elder observed that Gauls and Iberians leavened their dough with the "foaming head of their ale," producing, he wrote, "a lighter kind of bread than other people's." Which came first, the pint or the loaf? It remains a mystery.

"The history of bread," wrote Piero Camporesi in *The Bread of Dreams: Food and Fantasy in Early Modern Europe*, "is the dietary expression of a long battle between the classes." In ancient Rome

At the outset of the French Revolution, Marie-Antoinette is reputed to have declared, "Let them eat cake!" when informed that the peasants had no bread. It sounds likely, but there's no evidence that the callous French queen ever uttered the words. If she did, historians suggest she probably said "Let them eat brioche." The price of baguettes was pegged to keep them affordable for the poor. If French bakers ran out, they were obligated to sell the buttery, eggy brioche at the baguette price.

RICE: A CULTURE'S DESTINY

Author Vertamae Grosvenor, filmmaker Julie Dash, and poet Nikky Finney have more in common than their professions as accomplished writers and story-tellers. As descendants of African slaves brought to the lowlands and sea islands of South Carolina and Georgia to cultivate rice, the three women also share the rich culture that anthropologists call Gullah, but they call Geechee. They've gathered in the home of Julie's uncle, John T. Dash, or Uncle Johnny, to prepare a meal and talk about their common bond.

"Rice came here because skilled Africans were brought here to grow rice to make South Carolina incredibly, indisputably rich. And so it's not just a grain of food . . . it's gold. In its day it was gold," says Finney.

Rice is also a seminal feature of Geechee culture. Largely isolated from mainstream America, the Geechees were able to preserve and adapt many aspects of their West African heritage, including language and crafts traditions. Yet their rice-based cuisine seems to be what sets them apart.

At the sink in Uncle Johnny's spacious kitchen, Dash runs water into a colander of rice and scrubs the grains. "I think what made us different was that we always had rice with every meal," she says, looking up as she continues swishing the rice. "Before the meal was being planned or whatever, a pot of rice was put on the stove."

As she sorts fresh greens, Vertamae Grosvenor recalls that after her family left South Carolina for Philadelphia, she felt marginalized by her heritage, as if it were something to be ashamed of. She recalls a schoolmate who derisively labeled her "one of them bad-talking, rice-eating Geechees from South Carolina."

Grosvenor laughs ironically as she tells how she used to insist to anyone who would listen that her family ate potatoes or spaghetti—*anything* but rice, which is, in fact, what they ate every day. She swore to never bear that stigma again. "I said, *When I grow up I'm not going to have rice in my kitchen and you could open my refrigerator you wouldn't see no rice pot.*"

But all three women have come to grips with their Geechee culture and have gone on to celebrate their heritage through memoirs, novels, poetry, and films. And they have come to prize the making of a proper pot of Geechee rice. For this get-together, Dash is making red rice the way her aunt Gertie taught her.

"I have a traumatic experience that has stayed with me," she tells her friends. "All the family was over. I guess it was a Sunday or something and I was gonna make the red rice. And after my aunt Gertie instructed me on how to wash the rice three times and then one more time for good luck, you know, we put the rice in a pan and then I kind of walked back into the kitchen and opened the pot and began to stir it."

She pauses for effect. "And then I heard this shriek and I turned around and everyone was screaming, 'Oh my God! She opened the pot! She's stirring the rice!' For years I heard about that. You know, you're never supposed to put a spoon or fork in the rice, once it starts to boil."

Dash shares another family cooking tip. When the rice is on the stove, she lifts the lid, places a piece of brown paper bag on the pot, and replaces the lid, now fitted with a steamproof seal. "This is my grandmother's tip for cooking red rice," she explains.

While the rice cooks, Uncle Johnny prepares another family favorite. "They would tell the children it is called Son of a Gun," Julie remembers, "but it is really called Son of a Bitch because it is so hot."

Johnny liberally shakes the bottle of Tabasco sauce over the baking dish as he recites the ingredients. "Well, you got your eggs, and your eggplant, and then you have onions, green pepper, celery, garlic and Tabasco sauce, pepper and salt and just a dash of sugar. Just a dash. And of course after that's all together you put your shrimps in."

When the food is ready, the group lights candles, pours the wine, and takes seats at a table overlooking the Ashley River. Dash expresses disappointment that her rice isn't perfect, but no one seems to mind.

"If I'm eating rice," says Grosvenor, "I'm home."

ABOVE FROM LEFT TO RIGHT: Julie Dash washes the rice. John T. Dash adds the final touches to his dish, Son of a Gun. Julie wraps the pot lid in brown paper. Uncle Johnny and Julie enjoy the fruits of their labor.

Aunt Gertie's Red Rice

Serves 4

In South Carolina's lowlands and islands, the Geechee (or Gullah) have held on to their African identity: speaking their native dialect, keeping alive a rich artistic heritage, and eating rice with every meal. Filmmaker Julie Dash shares her recipe for making Geechee red rice the way her aunt Gertie taught her.

Place the rice in a large bowl of water and scrub it between your hands. Keep changing the water until it is clear of starch. Pour off the water.

In a deep, heavy pot with a lid, cook the bacon (or smoked turkey) in the vegetable oil. Add onions, peppers, and garlic, and cook until done. Add the tomato sauce and water mixture and bring to a boil.

When the mixture begins to boil, add the rice. Use a fork to make sure the rice is evenly distributed. When the rice begins to boil, do not stir it ("Never put a spoon in rice that's cooking"), lower the heat, and wrap a piece of wet brown paper bag around the lid of the pot and cover. Slow-cook until the rice absorbs all the sauce. "Every grain must stand on its own. Every grain must be red."

Red rice tastes even better the next day.

1 cup South Carolina white rice (do not use converted rice)

5 strips bacon (or substitute smoked turkey)

1/4 cup vegetable oil

1/2 cup chopped onions

1/2 cup chopped bell peppers

1 clove garlic, chopped

1/2 cup tomato sauce mixed with 1 1/2 cups water

emperors gave out free grain to almost a third of the populace, invoking Juvenal's sneer that the masses cared only for "bread and circuses." Feudal European lords later saw to it that peasants and villagers got enough bread to keep them alive. These power brokers were nobody's fools: Whenever peasants starved, revolution followed.

In the Middle East and on the Indian subcontinent, most breads come off a griddle rather than out of the oven. So-called flat breads originated with nomadic peoples—pinch off a lump of fresh dough and grill it when you stop to make camp. All the flat breads are culinary cousins, but over thousands of years they've taken on local characteristics. Middle Eastern pita and lavash are usually yeast-raised doughs quickly grilled to make them puff up with an air pocket in the middle. Indian roti is made without the yeast, but puffed over a hotter fire. Each flat bread is as different from the next as French bread is from a loaf of pumpernickel.

The Berbers of North Africa make flat breads, but they put wheat flour to even subtler uses by reconstituting a "grain" from coarse flour. Rub-bing semolina flour with damp fingers over a sieve causes the gritty little grains of durum wheat to clump together. Once each clump is half the size of a grain of rice, it's ready to be steamed over a boiling pot of meat or vegetable broth, called tagine. The traditional product—far more ethereal in texture and nuttier in flavor than commercial substitutes—is couscous.

Steaming wheat is one alternative to baking. Boiling it is another. Noodles made from wheat, with or without eggs, have been a part of northern Chinese home cooking for thousands of years. Although some scholars cite Arabic traders as introducing pasta to the West, folk wisdom has it that Marco Polo brought the idea of noodles back from his thirteenth-century sojourn in the court of the Great Khan. Certainly Italy came to be China's chief world rival in its devotion to noodles. Other parts of Europe may have developed their characteristic noodle dishes—German spätzle, for example, or the filled Polish pierogi—but no one can rival the Italians for sheer inventiveness with a little flour, an egg, and boiling water.

Couscous is the spiritual food of North Africa. A Friday-afternoon bowl of couscous, served after prayer, ceremonially ends the workweek. North Africans attribute *baraka* (good luck) and God's blessing to a dish of couscous. Folk tradition says that a woman can ensure her husband's fidelity by serving couscous in which she has hidden the tender bits of sheep's tail.

Cornucopia

While Europe and Asia were getting by on wheat, barley, and rice, the people of Mesoamerica were domesticating and improving maize (or corn, as it's known in North America). The classic breads made from corn—grilled tortillas and steamed tamales—remain central in the daily diet in Mexico and Central America, where corn was first domesticated about 5,600 years ago. Around 3,500 years ago, the people of the southern coast of Guatemala began soaking dried corn in water mixed with wood ashes to produce *nixtamal*, a Nahuatl (Aztec) word for the masa or dough used in making tortillas and tamales. Not only did the weak lye solution remove the hard husk from dried corn, but it also changed the chemistry of the amino acids to make corn a better source of complete protein, especially when combined with beans.

It took roughly 2,000 years for corn to spread to New England and southeastern Canada. Wherever corn took root, so did the people. Hunter-gatherers became at least part-time farmers because corn provided a food supply that could be stored from one growing season to the next. Villages grew up around corn patches, and populations burgeoned. As in Mexico, corn became central in the religions of Native Americans from the present-day Southwest to New England. Pueblo Indian folklore says that the Creator fashioned the people from corn dough. Other Native American legends say that Crow brought the people their first corn and beans, carrying one in each ear.

When Christopher Columbus bumped into the Americas, he "discovered" corn in the Bahamas and Cuba. He sent seeds back to Spain in 1494; they spread like wildfire across Europe and into Asia. By the mid-sixteenth century maize had debuted in China, where early records call it *hsi fan mai*, or "Western barbarian wheat." Today China is second only to the United States in corn production.

Maize reached the British Isles around 1600. The Pilgrims certainly recognized corn; they made off with a cache of it that they discovered on Cape Cod before they settled in Plymouth. Because the crop was so easy to grow, corn bread, mush, grits, hominy, spoonbread, dodgers, cornpone, cracklin' bread, and Indian pudding quickly became colonial staples. During his 1765–66 sojourn in London, Benjamin Franklin wrote to the *London Gazetteer* that "Indian corn, take it for all in all, is one of the most agreeable and wholesome grains in the world . . . and that johny or hoecake, hot from the fire, is better than a Yorkshire muffin." Particularly in the American South, where wheat is hard to grow, corn became the cornerstone of home cooking. To this day many Appalachian families serve corn bread at every meal.

Tale of the Tubers

We take for granted the steaming, flaky flesh of a baked potato, the mound of mashed potatoes with gravy, the heap of crispy fries, toothsome potato gnocchi, or the soothing soft bite of kugel. But like corn, the potato is a relative newcomer to world cuisine. Europe got its potatoes from the Spanish, who developed a liking for the native *papas* of Peru when they established that Andean colony in the early sixteenth century. (The people of the Andes had been eating potatoes for at least 8,000 years at that point.) But the Spaniards hardly had a monopoly on the tuber. Portugal quickly distributed potatoes to West Africa and India. And by the eighteenth century, the peasants of most of Europe were consuming great quantities of spuds. Virtually every national cuisine of Europe has its specialty potato dish—

the *frites* of France and Belgium, the vinegared salads of Germany, fried potatoes with a piquant paprika sauce in Spain, dilled potatoes in Sweden . . . still, no European people is so firmly associated with the potato as the Irish.

Potatoes came to Ireland in the 1580s, and proved an apt crop for a land ravaged by endemic warfare. Battles might destroy a field of grain, but potatoes survived underground. A small plot, it was said, could produce enough to feed a family of eight with leftovers for the pig and cow—ensuring a little bacon and butter to dress up the spuds. Meager and monotonous, the potato nonetheless provided enough calories and supplemental protein, vitamins, and minerals to keep people alive.

In the cool and soggy summer of 1845, disaster struck across Northern Europe as fungal spores spread on the winds and potato crops wilted and rotted in the fields. From Ireland to Poland, peasants began dying from malnutrition and disease, giving rise to revolutions across Europe in 1848. But few places were as devastated as Ireland, where the blight continued through 1850. Ire-

The potato is America's most popular vegetable. We consume more than twice the amount of spuds as tomatoes, number two on the list. More than half the potatoes grown in the United States are processed into chips, instant potato products, or frozen potato products.

land's population dropped from eight million to five, small family landholdings were aggregated into larger estates, and Irish nationalism flared as English and Anglo-Irish landlords evicted tenant farmers unable to pay their rent. Up to a million Irish died, and two million more emigrated, mostly to England and the United States.

Colonial empires spread the potato far and wide, and it caught on swiftly in South Asia. It is as difficult to imagine Indian cuisine without potatoes as it is to imagine Neapolitan cooking without its distant nightshade cousin, the tomato. Moreover, the blight abated in Europe, and more resistant strains led to a resurgence of the potato. Today it is the fourth most valuable food crop in the world; many cultures consider it a native plant.

Other roots and tubers have long fed much of the tropical world—notably yams, taro, and manioc. The yam was well established in the Pacific Islands before it came to the Americas via the slave trade. (Americans frequently but incorrectly label orange sweet potatoes as yams, but they are entirely different species with different nutritional profiles.) When true yam is on the menu in the United States, it is usually in a Hawaiian or Brazilian restaurant. In parts of Melanesia, exchanges of immense tubers, often more than one hundred pounds, still play a role in courtship and marriage arrangements. The Hawaiian uhi (a somewhat smaller yam) is, by tradition, one of the sacred canoe plants that Polynesians carried with them in their daunting migrations. In west and central African cooking, fufu is as important as mashed potatoes are to Euro-American cooking. In central Africa, fufu is made with manioc; in western Africa, it's often made from a combination of pounded yams and plantains. In both places, it's cooked up to make it stiff enough to roll in a ball, make an indentation, and use the fufu to scoop up stew or sauce.

KALO OUR BROTHER

A lū`au is in full swing at the Ko`Olina Resort on O`ahu. The emcee, in a bright blue shirt and white lei, greets the revelers with a hearty "Aloha!" Musicians keep the beat as men and women perform traditional dances. Everyone gravitates to a buffet table laden with dishes—including a bowl of thin purplish paste garnished with orchid flowers.

"You could be anywhere else in the world and have rice and potatoes but where can you have poi?" asks Keith Horita, the CEO of Paradise Cove Lū`au. He answers his own question: "In Hawai`i."

As diners ladle small portions onto their plates, their reactions seem to be equally divided and rarely neutral. "It's good," say some, with a note of surprise in their voices. "No, it's not good," others counter, grimacing.

Horita is undeterred. "Although some of our visitors would rather not have it, we keep the poi on the menu because it helps to maintain the authenticity of the Hawaiian experience."

Poi may be a novelty for visitors to the lush islands, who often find it at best an acquired taste. But poi is an essential part of the diet for native Hawaiians. The Polynesians who reached these islands by canoe from the Marquesan Islands sometime before the sixth century brought the taro plant—kalo in Hawaiian—as one of their sacred canoe plants. It was as essential as the pigs, dogs, and sweet potatoes that are deeply ingrained in Hawaiian life. The kalo plant, however, is in some ways first among equals. It is such an integral part of the culture that Hawaiian myth declares it the first child of the ancient gods—and therefore the older brother of the Hawaiian people. "It's family to us," says Calvin Hoe, an educator and kalo farmer.

Fellow farmer Vince Dodge stands ankle deep in his kalo paddy, or lo`i, and harvests the roots. "Kalo is an extremely nutritious food," he explains. "When you take the kalo and you pound it into the poi, it never rots. So you have a food that enabled the ancestors to travel all across the Pacific without refrigeration, without canned goods. And if

you water down poi in a bottle, you can raise an infant on it."

As he prepares poi the traditional way—pounding a kalo root in a wooden bowl with a stone pestle—Hoe reaches back to more recent Hawaiian history. "When Captain Cook came to Hawai`i, about 200 years ago, people say that the population was about a million people. That was sustained mainly by kalo. The lands were covered with these kalo fields." But in the centuries following Captain Cook's arrival, the Hawaiian nation was devastated by disease and displacement—and the kalo paddies shrank to less than 500 acres as sugar and pineapple plantations siphoned off the running water essential to kalo cultivation.

When nutritionist Claire Hughes purchases her expensive pre-prepared poi in a modern grocery store, she can't help but notice the irony. "This valley was all kalo plants, and so if you go out there in the parking lot, you can see there is blacktop on a

huge amount of property here," she says. "We've given up the space that once grew taro."

Hoe, Dodge, and farmer Paul Reppun are among those responsible for the kalo cultivation revival that paralleled the 1970s renaissance in Hawaiian cultural awareness. Growing kalo requires "cold, fast-flowing water," says Reppun as he stands in his verdant green field, served by a rushing stream. "We're in competition with municipal usage for water. The amount of water we flow through our taro patches could flush a lot of toilets, and people resent the fact that we had that water flowing."

Reppun and his neighbor Hoe even won a lawsuit, forcing sugarcane and pineapple agribusiness plantations to stop diverting water that would otherwise naturally flow into their valley. "This plant fortunately has water rights," says Hoe. "Fighting for this water for twenty-five years and looking ahead forever to be fighting for this water—it takes a toll on a person's health. But taking care of this kalo plant is another kind of battle. It is another way of fighting."

Nutritionist Hughes understands that kalo nourishes the spirit as well as the body. "Taro itself represents the god Kāne. He is one of the most powerful gods. So when you eat it into your body, you take in the godlike qualities of Kāne. Taking these essences into your body at every meal is very similar to taking communion."

She reaches into the refrigerator case at the market and selects—what else?—a container of poi. "I eat poi every day for breakfast," she says.

ABOVE FROM LEFT TO RIGHT: Poi, a traditional staple of the Hawaiian diet. Calvin Hoe pounds kalo to make poi. Claire Hughes buys packaged poi at the supermarket.

Another starchy root common to West Africa, the Caribbean, and the Pacific is taro, known in Hawai`i as kalo. Of all the sacred canoe plants, kalo has become a symbol of the Hawaiian people, and the most common preparation found in Hawai`i is poi. The recipe is the height of simplicity: Peel kalo root, cut it into pieces, and steam. When it's cool, mash with a pestle, adding water to thin the purplish paste to the desired texture. Poi has a significance beyond mere nutrition. It is a key dish at lū`aus celebrating such occasions as a high school graduation or first birthday. (Infant mortality used to be high in Hawai`i, making the first birthday a great cause for celebration.) People sit down to eat in a time of joy, and they eat poi.

In the Caribbean taro takes its place with several other roots and tubers as a starchy base for a wide range of prepared foods. In Cuba it is called malanga; in Puerto Rico, yautía. The Puerto Rican deep-fried fritters called alcapurrias are made from grated yautía mixed with mashed plantains and a leavening agent. Although rarely found outside the island, alcapurrias de juey— fritters stuffed with mangrove crabmeat—are a special delicacy. Crunchy on the outside, sweet and salty on the interior, a crab fritter is a long way from poi, but it is as quintessentially Puerto Rican as poi is Hawaiian.

Food for the Spirit

Not all cultures lean on cereal grains as the staff of life. East African pastoralists build their entire lives around herding cattle. Traditional Maasai of Kenya roam with their herds from pasture to pasture and water hole to water hole. Maasai mythology holds that the rain god Ngai made them custodians of all cattle in the beginning of the world when the earth and sky split. They have an almost mystical relationship with their herds, subsisting primarily on a diet of milk and cattle blood (drained from a small incision in the neck). The Maasai use cattle hides for mattresses and shoes, cattle dung for plastering the walls of their huts, sterile cattle urine for medicine. Only during periods of famine or on celebratory occasions do they slaughter an animal for meat.

In the Arctic and parts of northern North America, hunting cultures have a similarly close

Home of the annual Chitlin Strut (more than 10,000 pounds of chitlins consumed in one day): Salley, South Carolina

relationship with specific animals, and often define themselves by their quarry. Thus, many groups of Inuit consider themselves seal people—a relationship they once shared with the Hebrideans, whose intense prehistoric relationship with seals is preserved in the cycle of "silkie" legends about creatures who could change from seal to human and back. Until the late nineteenth century, Native Americans of the Great Plains were bison cultures. Their seasonal lifestyles revolved around hunting the American bison, which provided food, shelter, and a link to the spirit world.

In similar fashion, many of the woodland peoples of northeastern North America treated the white-tailed deer, elk, or caribou as their staff of life. Every scrap of a hunted animal had a use; waste was a spiritual affront to the sacred animal that had given its life. Hunting cultures that revolve around a single large animal are becoming scarce. The Sami people of northern Eurasia (formerly called Lapps) began to make the transition from hunters to pastoralists almost 5,000 years ago. The reindeer is their staff of life, but they have domesticated immense herds and use them not only as a source of food, shelter, and clothing, but also as beasts of burden. Along the rim of the northern Pacific Ocean, many of the indigenous cultures traditionally identify themselves as hunters—of seals, walrus, bears, and whales. Their struggles to assert traditional culture in the wake of modern international conservation measures are ongoing.

A WAY OF LIFE

Neah Bay, Washington, sits at the northwest corner of the United States across the Strait of Juan de Fuca from Vancouver Island. It is the home of the Makah or, in their own language, the Qwiqwidicciat: "people who live by the rocks and seagulls." For thousands of years the Makah ranged across the Olympic peninsula, always coming back to their rugged shore to hunt halibut and seals.

And gray whales, which migrate right past Neah Bay.

"Whaling was something that could be done by the most fit and prepared people that could actually feed a large segment of the community," explains Janine Bowechop of the Makah Cultural & Research Center. "Because whales are so large and can provide so much, they also allowed us to create a surplus of food that could be traded and stored. Whaling was very, very important as a food source—more important even than fish and seals."

In fact, whaling and its by-products—meat, blubber, and oil—were so important to the Makah that they made a fateful trade in 1855. In a treaty with the United States, the Makah gave up more than 90 percent of their land for the right to continue whaling. Soon after, commercial whalers hunted the gray whale to near extinction. By the 1920s the Makah had stopped whaling, but they never stopped thinking of themselves as a whaling people.

Even today the Makah remain deeply, spiritually tied to the sea. "When the tide's out, basically the table is set," explains tribal member Theron Parker. "We eat seals, clams, salmon, halibut, black cod, just anything pretty much that comes from the ocean."

His wife, Polly McCarty, concurs. "Everything here kind of revolves around food. It is just all connected, and food is connected. You know, you pray to go out and hunt the whale. You pray to go out and hunt the seal, you pray for a good season of salmon. Food is just part of that circle."

Thanks to a nearly worldwide halt to commercial whaling, the Pacific gray whale population

rebounded to 20,000 in the early 1990s. "Many of the whaling families of today," says Keith Johnson of the Makah Whaling Commission, "kept their traditions alive with their family songs, dances, and prayers." In 1994 the whales were removed from the endangered species list, and the Makah decided to enforce their treaty rights and resume the whale hunt—and their traditional way of life.

"Whale meat connects us with our grandparents and our great-grandparents," says Bowechop. "It's not just about food and it's not just about spiritual strength and it's not just about culture. It's really about the connection of all of those."

The Makah needed time to prepare for their first gray whale hunt in seventy years. Parker explains that they worked out to emulate their ancestors, paddling in long cedar dugout canoes two and three times a day. "We sacrificed a lot of things in our lives to be there, to be in that canoe. We sacrificed jobs,

relationships." And it changed them. "I gained my sobriety. I quit doing everything, you know, any kind of drugs or alcohol . . . I even quit drinking coffee. I just wanted to be part of that canoe."

On May 17, 1999, the conditions came together: The seas were calm enough to paddle, and a female gray whale had been spotted reasonably close to shore. The Makah fasted and prayed and made ready. The wives of the whalers readied themselves to remain still.

"As long as they were on the water I would have to not move," says McCarty. "It is the connection between the woman and the whale. If the whaler's wife is moving around, the whale will be that way also, and it could be dangerous for the men."

Protestors swarmed to the reservation, only to be rebuffed by tribal police. Self-styled protectors of the whales buzzed around the Makah canoe in fast little boats. They shouted epithets and called

ABOVE FROM LEFT TO RIGHT: Crab, just one of the types of seafood in the Makah diet. Octopus cooks in the kitchen of Polly McCarty and Theron Parker. Theron carves a paddle. This meal includes whale meat, in the blue bowl. More bounty from the sea. Polly and Theron prepare dinner.

for abolishing the treaty. They held up signs: SAVE A WHALE. HUNT A MAKAH.

But the Makah dug in their silent oars and closed on the gray whale. Theron Parker stood up and launched the harpoon—just as his great-grandfather had harpooned whales many decades earlier. It struck home. Blood blossomed in the water. Immediately, they shot the whale in the head to give her a humane death.

"It is ironic," says Bowechop, "that people focus so much attention on us very respectfully and in our traditional way taking very few whales, when this country consumes so much beef and chicken that is grown and slaughtered in really horrible conditions."

Parker speaks quietly of the experience. "You know you feel a lot of remorse for the whale because you're taking such a great life. But we pray for a long time to become the thunderbird to be able to use the lightning snake to take the whale home."

The successful whalers brought their quarry home, and the men of the village lashed ropes around the whale and pulled it up onto the beach to deafening cheers. The Makah prayed over the whale. They prayed for the whalers. And then they began to parcel out the flesh of the leviathan.

"The biggest thrill in my life was to feed fresh whale to my grandson and just to know that I didn't get this when I was a baby but my grandson is getting it," says McCarty. "To experience something that my ancestors went through is . . . There's no word to put to it."

The Makah have postponed further hunts until legal challenges to their whaling rights are resolved in the courts. But Theron Parker knows the Makah will never be the same. "It's made a big difference in our lives," he says. "We've all become a lot stronger. We're not just getting food for the mouth, but for the heart and for the mind and the spirit and everything."

ABOVE FROM LEFT TO RIGHT: Drumming at Theron Parker's house. The 1999 whale hunt. Makah paddlers.

FOOD RULES

It's "as French as frog's legs," "as American as apple pie." Our cuisine tells the world about us: our values, our class and gender structures, our beliefs. Specific foods, methods to prepare them, and the proper way and time to eat them are often the last things that individual cultural groups surrender in the process of assimilation. Generations after their ancestors arrived in America, Japanese Americans continue to eat mochi, or pounded sweet rice, on New Year's. Italian Americans living in Utah continue to enjoy rispelli, a sweet, deep-fried bread beloved in their native Calabria. At Christmastime Finnish Americans continue to make pulla, a cardamom-scented coffee cake. These foods carry with them memories of home, an ancestral past, and a continuation of unspoken cultural values.

Out of the incredible range of edible substances, each culture has developed its own rules of what is and isn't food. While Europeans and Americans are aghast to discover a fly in their soup, other people around the world find insects tasty and nutritious. The Ru Yang Boda Scorpion Breeding Company in Luoyang, China, employs thirty workers to raise three million scorpions in a facility the size of a football field. Some Chinese like to fry and serve them atop crisp rice

noodles. Other households prefer to mix river worms with eggs and bake them in a casserole, or stir-fry silkworm larvae with vegetables. When honored guests visit the Zapotecs of the Mexican state of Oaxaca, they are greeted with bowls of roasted grasshoppers tossed in hot chili powder and glasses of homemade distilled cactus juice, often bottled with a worm.

So strong are our unconscious rules about what is and isn't food that we perform mental gymnastics to accommodate new circumstances. When Christopher Columbus landed in the New World, he sought (and found) the familiar in the unfamiliar. On October 21, 1492, he and his men explored Fortune Island in the Bahamas. In his logbook Columbus recounted his amazement at the lush environment and expressed confidence

that many tasty delights awaited on the trees and bushes in this strange new world. Suddenly his exploratory party came upon something he had never seen: a giant iguana. They promptly speared the creature, roasted it, and dined. The explorer wrote, with obvious relish and not a trace of irony, "The meat is white and tastes like chicken."

Tastes like chicken—it's a phrase we still use to make mystery meat palatable. Snake. Lizard. Guinea pig. Rabbit. If the flavor is stronger and the flesh is dark (ostrich, emu, buffalo), "It tastes a little like beef." If it's greasy (tapir, armadillo, bear, raccoon), "It tastes like pork." In his account of the Plymouth Colony, William Brad-

ford related the events of January 4, 1621. The Pilgrims had run through their supplies and were beginning to starve. Miles Standish led an expedition to a nearby Native village to inquire about food but found the place deserted. "As they came home," Bradford wrote, "they shot at an Eagle and killed her, which was excellent meat. It was hardly to be discerned from Mutton." Similarly, Nantucket whalers sometimes harpooned and feasted on dolphins and porpoises as respite from a diet of fish. They called the cetaceans "sea pigs." "It is agreeable and tastes like pork," one captain recorded in his log.

Those encounters with iguanas, eagles, and

Neophobia

Human beings are funny about food. While we sometimes embrace novelty, we can also be neophobic, or resistant to new things. Anthropologists say both responses have been bred into us over the ages. It's a tricky wager—eat that weird stuff and evade starvation, or avoid it and escape being poisoned. Dodging potential poisoning is what scientists call bait shyness, the natural response codified in the folk saying *Once burned, twice shy*. Get sick on a dish once and you may never eat it again.

Bait shyness is often manifested on a broader scale in dietary laws. Cultural food taboos generally describe the prohibited food as "unclean"—either literally or spiritually poisonous. The Jewish dietary prohibitions in the book of Leviticus, subsequently adopted by Islam, labeled unclean many foods that other people readily ate. The twelfth-century Andalusian scholar Maimonides hypothesized that pigs were on the list because pork spoiled quickly in hot climates and carried disease from the animal's habit of rooting in garbage. But that logic should have also banned goats and, for that matter, cattle, both of which carry anthrax. In truth, the pig was only one of many animals banned by Jewish law, including camels, vultures, and rabbits. Pork attained special

dolphins were repeated over and over as hungry people made what they had conform to what they knew. It may have been mystery meat on the plate, but they prepared it, seasoned it, and sat down to eat it by the same principles of cuisine they would have employed with more familiar foods. Nor did the strangeness of eating iguana or eagle deter the Europeans. As they pressed farther into the North American wilderness, they found huge flocks and herds of animals, from passenger pigeons that turned the sky black to bison that made the earth shake. That astonishing abundance set Americans on a path to become the most carnivorous people in the world.

appeal outside the Jewish community, which used its dietary regulations as a way of setting Jews apart in the Roman world. The fledgling Christians pointed instead to the book of Matthew in the New Testament: "Know and understand; it is not what goes into the mouth that defiles a man, but that which comes out."

People who commonly eat a food that is taboo in another culture often consider the ban a matter of superstition. Burger-chomping Americans express incomprehension over the sacred status of cattle in India, where the 1947 constitution spells out the rights of cows. Yet those same Americans would never think of eating whale, monkey, dog, cat, or parrot. Our culture considers eating sentient or companion animals the next thing to cannibalism, perhaps the deepest food taboo of all.

status in 165 B.C. when the Syrian monarch Antiochus I slaughtered pigs in the Temple of Solomon and demanded that the Jews eat the flesh as a token of submission to his rule. Enraged, Judas Maccabeus organized an army that retook Jerusalem and reestablished the Temple, the triumphant revolt celebrated at Hanukkah. Thereafter, observant Jews demonstrated their moral purity and ethnic pride by shunning the pig.

Among major world religions Christianity is unusual in not espousing dietary laws. It was a deliberate choice by the founders of the institutional church, who were seeking to broaden their

Still, hunger trumps most taboos and food prejudices. When German armies laid siege to Paris in 1870, cutting off the city from the farms and gardens of the countryside, bourgeois restaurants offered such delicacies as rat ragù and saddle of cat. *Le même goût du poulet*, the waiters no doubt intoned. *Tastes just like chicken.*

Main entry point for the more than seven million pounds of durian shipped to the United States each year: Los Angeles

No Durians Allowed

UWAJIMAYA
KING of THE FRUITS
$7.99 /LB
FRESH DURIAN
NOT FROZEN

DURIAN FOR DUMMIES

In different cultures and different regions, everybody thinks what they eat is normal. It makes sense in the context of where they come from, who they are, and what's important to them. But some delicacies are clearly an acquired taste—like the durian. Popular in Southeast Asia, this prickly fruit related to the pineapple and papaya is now available in the United States.

Not everyone thinks that's a good thing.

The durian is reputed to be an aphrodisiac—hence the old Malaysian adage, *When the durian goes down, the sarongs go up*. But don't try to bring one through U.S. Customs—or even on a bus ride in Indonesia. Authorities there ban the durian from public transportation because it has such a strong odor, sometimes likened to garbage, sewage, or spoiled meat.

The custardlike interior takes some getting used to. Novice durian tasters liken the texture to scrambled eggs or custard and the taste . . . well, sweet but sour, or a little like garlic, or . . . "indescribable."

THE CREATION OF AN AMERICAN CUISINE

American cuisine was decades in the making—centuries, actually. Many cultural critics have argued that for the longest time, we Americans weren't quite sure who we were. If we couldn't agree on a national identity, how could we agree on a national cuisine? Americans long took a dim view of the way "foreigners" ate. For decades we sought to convert newcomers not just to the English language but to the Anglo-American table as well. During the late nineteenth century, settlement houses offered classes teaching

immigrant women how to cook the American way: well-done beef, green beans boiled gray with a piece of salt pork, and a nice heaping pile of mashed potatoes. One can only imagine the reaction of newly landed cooks from Sicily and Estonia.

The Victorian years saw anti-immigrant health campaigns sweep the Jewish pushcart vendors from New York City's streets and the chili queens from San Antonio's public plazas. By the 1920s domestic science and home economics courses in public schools actively discouraged one-pot meals ("hinders the digestion") and prescribed a diet based on colonial New England cooking: lots of codfish, white cream sauces, and mashed potatoes. For something fancy, they added Waldorf salad. Chinese immigrants and Native Americans were exhorted to drink milk, Mexicans to cast away their tortillas in favor of wholesome white bread, Italians to eat proper roasts, Poles and Jews to stop chomping dill pickles on the grounds that they were "injurious to the urinary tract." Even in the more politically correct twenty-first century, federal nutritional guidelines still presume a meal composed in the Northern European fashion of separate piles of meat, vegetables, and starch, as enshrined by sectioned cafeteria trays.

But Americans are notorious for turning a deaf ear to authority, and good food ultimately triumphed over bad theories. Although many urban immigrants adopted the bland menus of their American neighbors—except for holidays, weddings, funerals, and other special occasions—many others kept their Old Country dishes simmering away on the stoves of ethnic neighborhoods. To those grandmothers in Little Italy, Brooklyn, Germantown, Little Beirut, Chinatown, and Frenchville, we owe the pasta, matzoh balls, pancakes, shish kebab, chow mein, chowder, and other delights that have long since entered the mainstream American diet.

Other immigrants shunned the cities and dispersed to the hinterlands, where they tended to congregate with like-minded folks. Over the generations they lost their mother tongues and their accents, but their recipe boxes enriched the American table. Long before the emergence of a national cuisine, pockets of the United States began to develop full-fledged regional cuisines—not just a handful of specialties, but comprehensive bodies of complementary foods and ways to eat them.

The rural cotton South gave us Soul Food, a cuisine based to no small extent on the parts of the hog that the master sent to the slave quar-

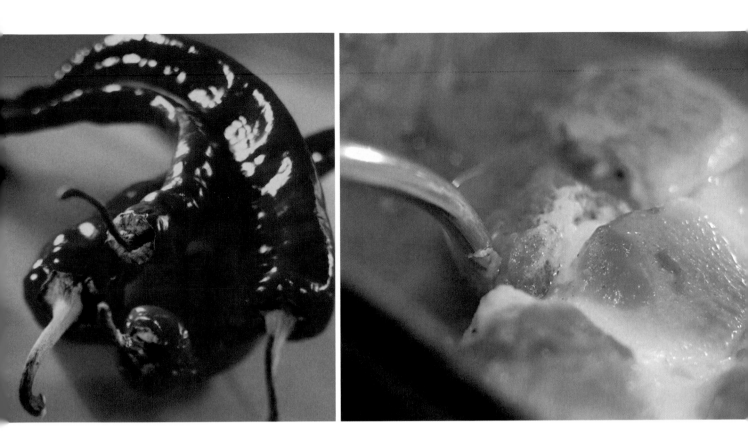

ters. Hocks and chitlins, trotters and snouts, all with a huge side of braised collard greens—it was a cuisine familiar in many parts of the world where people eat swine. But nowhere else were the pork parts supplemented with corn bread, batter-fried chicken, catfish, and rice with field peas. When folks left the rural South for the big northern cities, they brought their cooking with them. It was part of who they were, and many a garden patch in the North sprouted collards, black-eyed peas, and even sweet potatoes.

Possibly the most complex—and, to European tastes, most gourmet—of the early regional American cuisines is Louisiana Creole and its backwoods cousin, Cajun. Crawfish may swim in almost every freshwater stream in North America, but it took the people of the bayous to elevate them to the level of delicacy. The cuisine is replete with gumbos and étouffées and other sophisticated dishes that represent the best of American cultural fusion—African okra and rice, Native American sassafras, Spanish tomatoes and paprika, French techniques (and names), and a little bit of everything that swims, flies, creeps, grazes, pecks, or hops in the vast delta of the Mississippi River and the nearby Gulf of Mexico.

KOLACHES: A BITE OF CZECH TRADITION

Growing up as a child of Czech heritage, Bernard Rychlik recalls, "You would be called a sauerkraut-eater or something of that nature, and you would wear maybe clothes that were more of a farm-type thing, and you would get teased about that." He continues, "Of course it never bothered me none. You know, I was pretty good size. I could handle my own."

Today Rychlik is the mayor of Caldwell, the self-proclaimed Kolache Capital of Texas, where about a quarter of the county's population has a Czech background. They are the descendants of farmers who fled political upheaval and crop failures in the mid-nineteenth century to start new lives on the rich soil of south-central Texas. They have put the teasing behind them, choosing instead to celebrate their heritage through language, music, dance—and, of course, food.

As a festival approaches, Bernard's brother Joe Rychlik outfits himself in a white shirt and black vest trimmed with red braid to visit a group of second-graders. "I'm here to tell y'all about the big party we're having in Caldwell this weekend—the Kolache Festival. One of the events at the Kolache Festival is called the bake show. And what it is—ladies or men, children, they bake kolaches." He's referring to that Czech specialty, airy yeast-raised buns with sweet or savory fillings.

Retired baker Lydia Vajdak Faust is something of a kolache expert. She pulls a pan from the oven and deftly wields a big brush to glaze the top with butter. "The farmers were in the field, and women were also in the field. After they did housework in the morning, they were in the field along with the men. So they were busy during the week. Usually on Sunday or Saturday afternoon you would make kolaches." In fact, many an adult still has fond memories of midafternoon snacks of kolaches at Grandma's house on Sunday.

As members of the younger generation prepare their contest entries, they seem determined to carry on the culinary tradition. In their home kitchen Dana Yezak and son John carefully study a recipe.

John beats the egg, adds ingredients to a mixer, and then kneads the dough by hand. "If a boy wants to bake, let him bake!" he asserts. "If a girl wants to play football, let her play football! I mean, come on! It's a free country!"

Dana shares her son's enthusiasm. "Participating in the Kolache Festival just came out of the blue. And here we are in the middle of football schedules trying to achieve his goal of getting into the Kolache Festival," she says. "Whether we win or not, we're gonna make a good kolache, and we'll have something good to eat here at home with the leftovers. So that's all right with us."

In the Orsak kitchen, kolache baking is a three-generation effort. "My grandmother always baked kolaches, and my mother, so that's where I learned," Ella Orsak says as she works with her grandson Josef Orsak and his mother, Sheila. After arranging balls of dough on a baking sheet, Ella expertly makes indentations. Josef spoons in the filling.

On the morning of the contest, Josef sits in the backseat of his father's car. He is philosophical. "I don't expect to, you know, win like first place this year because there's a lot of people that enter and, you know, chances of getting it are very slim. So we'll just find out, I guess."

At 8:15 A.M. Josef joins a stream of youngsters gingerly carrying trays of kolache to the registration desk. By 9:30 baker Lydia Vajdak Faust, dressed in a traditional Czech folk costume with a garland in her hair, instructs the judges. "Think about—would you want to buy this kolache? Would you want to enter this kolache if it was yourself?" But she adds a cautionary note. "Don't judge them too harshly. Get them to enter next year again. That's what we're striving for, these younger ones to take up their culture. The older bakers are fading out fast."

As festivalgoers dance, listen to music and engage in a kolache-eating competition (the winner devours eight in seventy-eight seconds), the judges do their job. They inspect the pastry, breaking off small pieces and chewing thoughtfully.

It's hard to tell whether the adults or the children are more nervous as they sit in the stands and wait for the results. "There is a top kolache in each of the eleven classes," says announcer Ann Sebasta at last. "The top kolache in each class is the one that gets the rosette."

When his name is called in the apricot class, Josef Orsak rushes to the podium to receive his ribbon and a bag of flour. He also gets a big hug from his grandmother. "I'm so proud, I want to cry," says Ella Orsak.

ABOVE FROM LEFT TO RIGHT: Ella Orsak and grandson Josef put the finishing touches on their kolaches. Brothers Bernard and Joe Rychlik are enthusiastic supporters of the Kolache Festival.

Kolaches

CLAUDIA MATCEK'S KOLACHES

2 packages dry yeast

¼ cup warm water

1 tablespoon sugar

2 cups milk

½ cup butter or margarine

½ cup sugar

2 teaspoons salt

5¼ cups sifted flour

2 egg yolks, slightly beaten

1 cup sifted flour

In Caldwell, Texas, the local Czech-American residents and their neighbors consider making kolaches an art form, and the kolache bake show gives area children and adults a chance to display their craft. There, kolaches are judged in eleven categories according to type of filling, including cream cheese, poppy seed, apricot, apple, cherry, strawberry, peach, prune, and sausage. Below, Claudia Matcek (a Texas Kolache Grand Champion) shares her recipe for kolaches and poppy seed filling with glaze, while Mildred Gaas contributes her recipe for cream cheese filling. Recipes are courtesy of the Burleson County Czech Heritage Museum.

CLAUDIA MATCEK'S KOLACHES

Dissolve yeast in the warm water. Stir in 1 tablespoon of sugar and let stand.

Heat milk in a saucepan until it's pretty hot to touch, almost scalding. Remove from heat and stir in butter or margarine and ½ cup sugar. Cool to lukewarm and add yeast mixture.

In a large bowl combine salt and 5¼ cups flour. Add the yeast and milk mixture and mix well. Mix in egg yolks. Add enough of the last cup of flour to achieve the desired texture (to make it workable, not too sticky, so it can be removed from the bowl and kneaded). Most of the time, I use the whole cup.

Knead dough on a floured board until glossy. Grease a large bowl. Put dough in bowl and roll it around to grease the surface. Cover the bowl and let the dough rise in a warm place until double in bulk.

Roll out dough to about ½ inch thick and cut into individual kolaches with biscuit cutter. Place on greased pan so they are not quite touching. Brush with softened butter or margarine and let rise again, covered, until light to touch.

Make indentation in each and fill with poppy seed filling (or another filling of your choice). Bake in a preheated 375-degree oven until brown, about 25 minutes. Remove and brush with softened butter or margarine.

CLAUDIA MATCEK'S POPPY SEED FILLING AND GLAZE

Heat milk to boiling point. Add sugar, flour, and poppy seeds, stirring vigorously. Cook over medium heat until mixture thickens. Remove from heat. Add butter or margarine and then the vanilla. Cool the filling before spooning about 1 teaspoon filling in the indentation in each kolache.

Glaze

Combine powdered sugar, margarine, vanilla, and milk over low heat. Spoon over kolaches while still warm.

MILDRED GAAS'S CREAM CHEESE FILLING

In a bowl place cream cheese, vanilla, egg, and sugar. Mix well together before filling kolaches.

CLAUDIA MATCEK'S POPPY SEED FILLING AND GLAZE

1¹/₂ cups milk

1¹/₄ cups sugar

1 tablespoon flour

1 cup ground poppy seeds

1 teaspoon butter or margarine

1 teaspoon vanilla

Glaze

2 cups powdered sugar

2 tablespoons margarine

¹/₂ teaspoon vanilla

4 tablespoons milk

MILDRED GAAS'S CREAM CHEESE FILLING

2 8-ounce packages cream cheese

2 tablespoons vanilla

1 egg

1 cup sugar

Ethnicity: The New Taste of America

American cuisine started to come together, ironically enough, with the reassertion of ethnic identities in the 1960s and 1970s. As historian Donna R. Gabaccia noted in *We Are What We Eat: Ethnic Food and the Making of Americans*, "Racial minorities instituted this ethnic revival . . . by demanding recognition for their unique histories and ways of life. The descendants of white southerners and immigrants from southern and eastern Europe soon joined the revival, and many considered themselves new ethnics."

Generic ethnic festivals took on new strength throughout the country. Oktoberfest became as much an occasion to eat sausages as to drink beer. St. Patrick's Day moved beyond parades and corned beef and cabbage to recall bacon rashers and champ (green peas and mashed potatoes). Chinese New Year centered as much on long-life noodles and Peking duck as firecrackers and dancing dragons.

To respond to this new awareness of cultural identity as expressed in food, culinary historian Elisabeth Rozin codified the seasoning combinations that serve as ethnic signatures in her 1973 *Flavor-Principle Cookbook*. Mediterranean Italian and French cooking, for example, are redolent with olive oil, tomato, garlic, and fresh herbs, usually thyme, rosemary, or basil. Some of Thailand's signature flavors are coconut, fish sauce, and lemongrass, while Cantonese cooks have a heavy hand with soy sauce, brandied wine, gingerroot, sesame and peanut oil, and garlic. Indian cooking is distinguished by the subtle and shifting blend of spices that the West calls "curry": garlic, cumin, ginger, turmeric, coriander, cardamom, and pepper. (The mix might also include mustard seed, saffron, cloves, coconut, or vinegar, depending on whether the dish is intended to be sweet, hot, or sour.) Mexican cuisine's signatures are tomato, dried ancho and fresh serrano chile peppers, cumin, and oregano. Indonesian and

related Malay kitchens lean on soy sauce, garlic, molasses, and peanuts. The very presence of dill or caraway in a dish points to Scandinavian or Russian origin. Rozin argued that immigrants might be forced to switch ingredients in a traditional dish, but they could preserve its essence with seasonings.

By the mid-1970s, heritage festivals with a major focus on ethnic foods began to proliferate. The Annual Feast of the Blessed Sacrament in New Bedford, Massachusetts, which was established in 1915, metamorphosed into the Portuguese Festa, the largest Portuguese ethnic celebration in the world. Each year it draws up to 300,000 people to feast on such delicacies as

carne de espeto (a form of barbecue), stewed codfish, marinated fresh tuna, carne guisada (stewed beef), stewed rabbit, fresh fava beans, sausages, and fried pastries. Klamath, California, created the mid-August Klamath Salmon Festival, with its Native American games and traditional salmon barbecue over an alder fire. Inspired by the Columbia Restaurant's annual giveaway of bean soup, Ybor City (part of Tampa, Florida) established its Cuban-American Ybor City Fiesta Day, complete with free servings of bean soup, café con leche, and Cuban bread. Midwesterners celebrate all things Scandinavian at the Nordic Fest in Decorah, Iowa, where lefse (potato-based griddle bread), rømmegrøt (sour cream por-

ridge), and smørbrød (open-faced sandwiches) are supplemented with such pastries as kringle, krumkaker, and sandbakkels. The chile-pepper-growing capital of Las Cruces, New Mexico, got into the act with the Whole Enchilada Festival, featuring cook-offs in red and green chile categories and the world's largest enchilada, made with 250 pounds of masa. The festivals of patron saints in Boston's North End, once the province of southern Italians, became a summerlong series of parades and Neapolitan, Sicilian, and Calabrian street food.

Ethnicity in America is no longer something to hide, but a heritage to explore. New Englanders have taken a fresh look at lobster and corn chowder. Country-style smoked hams have reappeared on southern holiday dinner tables. Even lutefisk—a pungent Scandinavian specialty of dried fish rehydrated in a caustic soda bath, then baked or pickled—became a hit across the Upper Midwest.

Hawaiian Poké

Serves 3 to 5

1 pound Ahi tuna, cut in
1-inch squares

³/₄ teaspoon Hawaiian sea salt

¹/₃ cup onion, diced

¹/₄ stalk green onion, chopped

¹/₂ teaspoon toasted sesame seeds

¹/₂ cup soy sauce

¹/₂ cup Ogo seaweed (green
seaweed), or substitute
1 tablespoon sesame oil and
1 teaspoon dried and chopped
chile peppers

Poké is a traditional Hawaiian dish that evolved with the influence of Japanese, Chinese, Korean, Philippine, Portuguese, and other cultures. Today poké is usually made with raw seafood cut into cubes and seasoned with spices and sauces. This version of poké, using raw tuna, is the easy way to make this favorite Local Food, explains Peter Buza, owner and chef of Kaua`i Family Restaurant in Seattle.

Mix all the ingredients in a bowl and marinate from 5 minutes to 1 hour.

Serve raw over lettuce leaves or chopped cabbage, or over a bed of crisp, fried bean threads.

LOCAL FOOD

The desert of Las Vegas, Nevada, is the antithesis of the lush Hawaiian Islands. But the city of neon-lit casinos backed by mountain peaks is sometimes called "the ninth Hawaiian Island." About 80,000 Hawaiians live and work in Las Vegas—and like newcomers everywhere they bring along a taste of home.

In their case, that taste is Local Food—an inclusive kind of cuisine that mixes and matches favorite dishes from indigenous Hawaiians and all the immigrant groups that settled on the islands. It's not hard to find this comfort food in Las Vegas, where restaurants advertise "Hawaiian plates" and radio deejays extol the virtues of Local Food.

The word goes out over the airwaves like a whisper in the night. "A word to the wise for all my Hawaiian brothers and sisters out there in the desert at the casinos. Whether you're here to gamble or live, we know where there's real Local Food—the food that says 'home' to us locals," one deejay tells his listeners. "Us mixed-up Hawaiian, Chinese, Filipino, Portuguese, Japanese, haole, Korean people from the great state of Hawai`i."

Whether in Las Vegas or back home on Mau`i, a Hawaiian plate lunch begins with "two scoops rice" and a serving of macaroni salad. Diners then might round out their plates with a selection of dishes that would do justice to a cafeteria at the United Nations: kalua pork (cooked Pacific-style in an underground oven), saimin (Japanese noodles in broth, topped with fish cake or scrambled egg), lomi salmon (cubes of salted raw fish with onion and tomato—also indigenous Hawaiian), or manapua (Chinese steamed buns, usually filled with pork, vegetables, or sweet beans). For a wallop the buffet offers kimchee, the potent Korean dish of pickled cabbage and hot peppers. For a sweet ending diners pick malasadas— Portuguese fried dough sprinkled with sugar.

"It's all *ono grinds*," says the deejay: "That is Hawaiian for 'good food'—even in Vegas."

ABOVE: Lance Kosaka, sous-chef at Alan Wong's Restaurant in Honolulu, prepares Local Food in Hawai`i. Lopaka and Barbara Strekow and family in front of their Bobbie's Grinds booth at the Hawaiian Civic Club/Pacific Islander Ho`olaulea, or Festival, in Las Vegas.

The Evolution of the American Restaurant

Concurrent with the resurgence of ethnic pride (and ethnic food), mainstream American cuisine has been undergoing a revolution based on inclusion instead of exclusion, as if we're all borrowing from our neighbors' recipe boxes. And a large part of the new American food culture over the last three decades has been happening in our restaurants. With the culinary revolution of the 1970s, the restaurant suddenly became central to how we ate, and with whom. The extended family was on the decline—so we went out to eat. All the adults in the household had jobs—so we went out to eat. A generation of noncooks came

of age—so we went out to eat.

After decades of domination by exclusive French cuisine, American restaurateurs like to point to the 1959 opening of Four Seasons in New York as the opening salvo of the American dining revolution. Owner Joe Baum printed all the menus in English, worked with cooking teachers and authors James Beard and Julia Child to develop menus around seasonal products, and introduced dining as an accessible but fine-arts experience. Flash ahead to 1971, when Alice Waters opened Chez Panisse in Berkeley, California. A student of French culture and literature, Waters reasoned that with the delicious products of California agriculture, there was no

reason she couldn't eat as well at home as she had in Paris. Her light and imaginative "California cuisine" not only swept the country, but also established beachheads all over the world through chefs who trained with her.

By 1980, when James Beard wrote *American Cookery*, he was confident enough to announce that "we have developed one of the more interesting cuisines of the world. It stresses the products of the soil, native traditions, and the gradual integration of many ethnic forms into what is now American cooking."

A new generation of chefs came on the scene—people who had fallen in love with cuisine on their travels and, increasingly, Baby Boomers who attended America's growing number of culinary schools. Perplexed about whether to call their restaurants French, Italian, Mediterranean, or even fusion, they billed their establishments as presenting New American food. In its most common incarnation, the New American restaurant employs the techniques of chef Auguste Escoffier to prepare local ingredients or put a contemporary spin on traditional dishes. The creative side comes in unexpected pairings—lettuce in the minestrone, grapefruit in the crab salad—and flavoring techniques assimilated from cuisines around the globe. Some critics have hailed the early twenty-first century as the golden age of American restaurants.

The creation of New American cuisine has another side, of course—in addition to the deliberate envelope pushers in the restaurant trade are the thoughtful home cooks to whom all those innovations and taste sensations trickle down, sometimes through food publications, sometimes through sheer curiosity about replicating a restaurant dish at home.

And increasingly, our dietary repertoire has come to represent American multiculturalism. Part of the credit for opening up the American palate goes to Frieda Caplan, who founded Frieda's Finest in 1962 as a supplier of what were then exotic foods. Caplan introduced Americans to kiwifruit, brown mushrooms, shallots, mangoes, and a range of other products that are now staples on grocery store shelves.

In *Why We Eat What We Eat*, culinary critic Raymond Sokolov mused, "From a social perspective the history of eating over the last five hundred years can be described as an international process in which the products and customs of all the different places and cultures in the world have become increasingly available to all people at all times." He was speaking about the dissemination of New World botanicals into Old World cuisines, but he could as well have been writing of the world market at the American gro-cery store and the open mind-set of New American diners.

That most American of fast-food institutions, the food court at the mall, may even best symbolize just who we are as a culture. Far from the forced fusion of concept chefs in the 1980s, who were capable of creating such abominations as Chinese-Italian "Ciao Mein," we take our ethnicities in discrete bites—Thai for lunch, Mediterranean for dinner, tomorrow maybe Korean. Eating functions much like travel, and if the American menu sometimes seems like the fourteen-day packaged tours of the 1960s (*If it's Tuesday, it must be Brussels*), at least we've all come to the smorgasbord. The ethnicity block on U.S. Census forms has grown increasingly complex over the years to slice and dice racial and cultural backgrounds into smaller and smaller bits. Yet even the Census offers a box that says "Other." Judging by the way we eat, perhaps there should be one more that says "All of the Above."

You are what you eat, said Charaka. We are the world.

FOOD & FAMILY

"You better come on in my kitchen, it's goin' to be rainin' outdoors," sang bluesman Robert Johnson between the pops and sliding whines of his bottleneck guitar. It was maybe the homiest image ever penned by a musician otherwise known for lyrics as sharp and dangerous as a broken whiskey bottle. "Come on in my kitchen . . ." It's an invitation to intimacy, the embrace of family, the gesture of a good friend, the summons to come on in and take a load off, literally or figuratively.

With the disappearance of fireplace cooking, the kitchen table has replaced the hearth. We sit down with friends for coffee or tea, a snack, and conversation. The family coalesces around the kitchen table as Mom cooks, Dad kibitzes, and the kids do their homework. Even more than in front of the television, the kitchen table is the nexus of the household, the place where families (born or chosen) engage and interact. Robert Johnson's invitation implies that whatever storm may be raging outside, in the kitchen we'll be safe and dry and warm.

Bonds are created and families defined by the small daily rituals of gathering, preparing, and consuming food. Parents and children play out their shifting roles, men and women perform their intricate gender dances, and families reaffirm—or strain—their bonds at the table. What's for dinner may be less important than who made it and who showed up to eat it. Every loving spoonful is weighted with the emotions of home, family, and relationships. As Oscar Wilde observed in *A Woman of No Importance*, "After a good dinner one can forgive anybody, even one's own relations."

FOOD AND GENDER

That invitation into the kitchen, Robert Johnson notwithstanding, almost always comes from a woman. Around the world and throughout history, preparation of the daily meal has been women's work. In countless societies, a woman's worth is measured to a good degree by her cooking skills.

"Can she bake a cherry pie, Billy boy, Billy boy?" goes the old Appalachian folk tune.

Running the kitchen carries the potential for great power. After all, our most basic drive—the need to eat—is never-ending, and it's mostly Mom who satisfies it. As Marcus Samuelsson explains, overwhelmingly, "a mother determines what, when, how much, and with whom the family eats. In giving us our daily bread or bowl of rice, a mother gives us not only her sustenance, but her beliefs, her worldview . . . and, of course, her love."

Mom also keeps us healthy. Writing in the *Journal of Gastronomy* in 1993, Lawrence Lindner concluded that dining alone "may contribute to the deterioration of the nutritional quality of our diets. People who eat alone follow poorer diets than those who eat with friends and family." We can learn a lot from other societies. The Japanese Dietary Guidelines for Good Health, for example, include the usual advice on limiting fats and calories and eating your vegetables. But they also exhort diners "to rediscover meals as pleasurable occasions and as opportunities for communication." In other words, with whom we eat is just as important as what's on our plates. Americans could do worse than to borrow the practice of the relaxed two-hour Mediterranean lunch.

The idea that American families no longer sit down to eat together contains more than a germ of truth, but a 1999 survey found that seven of ten American families gather for dinner at least five days a week. Three-quarters of the respondents to the survey said that family bonding is a top priority at mealtime and is enhanced by participation in every aspect of the meal, from planning to preparation to cleanup. Our hunger for family ties shines through. Eighty-nine percent said their family traditions are being forged at mealtimes, and more than half the respondents added that they would like to eat together more often and in a more relaxed atmosphere.

Ironically, the family dinner so sacrosanct in the folklore of mainstream American culture is a relatively recent phenomenon. The middle-class family dinner didn't exist in the early nineteenth century, when people grabbed meals when they could. The bourgeois dining room was still decades off, and most people ate their biggest meal at midday. According to historian John Gillis, writing in the *Journal of Family History* in 1996, "Dinner did not become a fixed time in a fixed place in Britain and America until the 1860s, where it has remained virtually unchanged right up until the present."

By and large women had always been stuck with the cooking, but at about the same time that dinner was enshrined in the early-evening slot, American gender roles also became more rigid. The woman of the house was expected to look after the physical, moral, and spiritual well-being of everyone under her roof. Social roles were changing, and many women sought guidance.

Literature directed at women blossomed in the United States during this period. The predecessors of *Ladies Home Journal* and *Good Housekeeping* (both of which launched in the 1880s) were full of advice about proper manners, proper cookery, and proper deportment. These magazines spoke to women who were often the first in

OBENTÔ

It's lunchtime at the bilingual Japanese-English Megumi Pre-School in Bellevue, Washington, and the children are full of energy. They sit down at the table and unwrap small plastic containers that have been tied—giftlike—in pieces of colorful fabric. They open each container to discover colorful morsels of food artfully arranged to resemble stars and soccer balls, watermelon slices and flowers, or the smiling faces of cats or pandas. After they have compared their luncheon fare with their classmates', they dig in with forks, chopsticks, and fingers.

"When we have obentô day, kids sit around the table, and they're not only excited about the food, but excited to share what their parents made for them," says teacher Yayoi Brown, referring to the elaborate lunches that Japanese women pack for their children to give them a reassuring sense of home as they negotiate the unfamiliar world of nursery school.

To Americans raised on peanut butter and jelly or tuna fish sandwiches, it's hard to imagine that a Japanese mother might spend up to an hour on an obentô box, making certain that it appeals to her child in both taste and appearance. Indeed, as one Japanese magazine noted, "The making of the obentô is one of the most worrisome concerns facing the mother of a child going off to school for the first time." An entire industry of cookbooks, containers, and other accessories supports this obligation, which many mothers regard as a measure of their creativity.

Despite its demands on their time, some Japanese-American women have adopted the tradition. "I have memories of my mother making obentô when I was little," says Brown. "I fortunately have a child who eats anything and everything. Hopefully when she grows up, she'll make obentô for her children, too, with the same kind of love."

their families to move from farm to town, from Old Country to New World. Native-born daughters of hardscrabble farmers or freshly landed from overseas, they sought to emulate the emerging, urbanized American middle class.

Catherine Beecher, sister of novelist Harriet Beecher Stowe, penned a series of books on cooking and housekeeping, all the while championing the rights and power of women. With great indignity, she demanded, "In what ways are women subordinate?" and proceeded to enumerate the unjust and inhumane ways in which women were deprived of legal standing. She also asked, "Wherein are they superior and equal in influence?" Her answer was cagier and more succinct: in moral authority, as the teacher of values in the household . . . and in the kitchen. Men were constitutionally unfit for the fine art of cooking, she concluded, but women could control the world from the stovetop.

The whole process of codifying domestic science achieved a full head of steam in the 1870s and 1880s, as popular cooking schools sprang up in New York, Philadelphia, and Boston. "Cook-

books" of the era set forth definitions of not just the proper table but also proper dress, grooming, and behavior. Such prescriptive books were aimed squarely at middle-class women; with fewer and fewer households able to maintain servants, the women of the house were forced to learn to cook. One of the most influential was the *Boston Cooking-School Cook Book* by Fannie Merritt Farmer, first published in 1896. Farmer is widely credited with making cooking a science as well as an art by insisting on precise measurements of ingredients. The wife, she reasoned, should be the chemist of the kitchen.

Some of Farmer's other innovations are still with us. She was a great believer in white sauce, and suggested its general use to coat meats or to reheat vegetables. She also favored salads of leftover tidbits encased in aspic or suspended in mayonnaise. Long after Mrs. Farmer has gone to the banquet table of the afterlife, we frequently say grace over a table laden with chicken in mushroom soup sauce and Jell-O salad with pineapple and miniature marshmallows.

Farmer could not have imagined the conven-

Since the Pillsbury Bake-Off began in 1949, more than 4,000 finalists have competed for the grand prize, which now carries an award of $1 million. In 1996 Kurt Wait of Redwood City, California, became the only male grand prize winner, with a recipe for Macadamia Fudge Torte.

ience foods that would burst into the American supermarket in the late 1940s, in no small part inspired by the technological advances food companies had made to supply rations to the troops during World War II. Dehydrated and reconstituted milk, potatoes, and soup mixes flooded the aisles. Frozen orange juice began to displace fresh squeezed—and it was available all year. Home economists at large packaging companies began to dream up hitherto unheard-of ways to combine their products, giving us the quintessential boxtop cuisine of the 1950s and early 1960s: macaroni-tuna bake, green bean casserole topped with crunchy onion rings, and undiluted canned cream soups to envelop a mélange of frozen and canned vegetables. As more and more women took on jobs outside the home (the numbers doubled between 1950 and 1960), *quick and easy* became bywords on the packages and on the covers of women's magazines.

U.S. leader in Jell-O consumption: Des Moines, Iowa

Back to the Future

For all the advances and upheavals the world has seen as it steps into the twenty-first century, Mom is still in charge of her family's nutritional and emotional well-being. Census figures from 2000 confirm the essential and ongoing truth: Although 60 percent of women hold down jobs outside the home, 77 percent of home meals are prepared by women without assistance from spouse or children. Indeed, a female-directed Pillsbury advertis-

ing campaign insisted that "Nothing says lovin' like something from the oven"—though it further hinted that cooking from scratch couldn't possibly be as good as cooking from the dairy case. ("Pillsbury says it best.")

Culinary historian Laura Shapiro has a droll take on cooking as "women's work" and the Pillsbury jingle. In *Something from the Oven: Reinventing Dinner in 1950s America*, she calls the association of women and meal preparation "something tantamount to a sex-linked characteristic. . . . Women have the babies, women feed the babies, women feed everyone else while they're at it; hence, women cook."

We all have our favorite family recipes, sometimes handed down from the Old Country, sometimes clipped from a newspaper or magazine. Gen-Xers get occasional cravings for old-fashioned (circa-1972) homemade granola, Baby Boomers grow nostalgic for their mothers' tuna melts, their mothers yearn for Aunt Bess's Lady Baltimore cake. Yet as more and more women (and many men) come to see cooking as an art as well as a necessity, the cookbook industry is on a roll.

According to industry sources, the *Better Homes & Gardens Cookbook* ranks behind only the Bible and the dictionary as the best-selling book in the world. Dog-eared and butter-stained

copies inhabit kitchens across the country. Since the first edition in 1930, the red-and-white-checked standard has sold more than thirty-four million copies. The industry as a whole is no less fruitful: In 2003 alone, total cookbook sales reached sixty million copies.

But commercial publishing only tells half the story. As early as the 1880s, churches and social clubs of immigrant groups began publishing Yiddish, Italian, Polish, and Russian recipe collections—at first in native languages, but usually in English after World War I. These descriptive cookbooks have rarely been about technique or culinary education—they are treasure boxes of grandmothers' recipes for cracklin' bread, latkes, ragù, pierogi, tamales, and a host of other ethnic specialties.

Following World War II the nature of these quintessentially American cookbooks shifted, as such women's organizations as the Junior League began issuing regional books to raise money for charity. Moms stepped forward with their personal versions of regional and family favorites, and their contributions were duly noted. Suddenly a woman's reputation as a good cook went beyond friends and family to the extended community who tried her recipes.

Forward to the Future

Mainstream American culture has long subscribed to the caveman notion of division of labor: It's the man's job to kill a beast and drag it home, the woman's job to cook it while he guards the fire. (Or reads the paper.) But times *are* changing. In households headed jointly by an adult male and adult female, a 1994 study found that men were involved with meal planning 23 percent of the time, shopping 36 percent, and food preparation 27 percent. These figures, the researchers noted, marked a significant rise from a similar study done two decades earlier.

When American men do get around to cooking, they often rely on flamboyance to make up for infrequency. In one of the last editions of her etiquette guide before her death in 1960, Emily Post observed, "To the old saying that man built the house but woman made of it a 'home' might

In 2004 Americans purchased 927,000 tons of charcoal briquettes and 98,500 tons of lump charcoal. We also burned our way through more than 15 million pounds of charcoal-flavoring wood chips, of which more than 8 million pounds were hickory and more than 6 million pounds were mesquite.

be added the modern supplement that woman accepted cooking as a chore but man has made of it a recreation."

Confirmed bachelor and lifelong gourmand James Beard did much to make it okay for American guys to rustle up some grub. After a first cookbook on hors d'oeuvres and canapés, Beard hit his manly stride with *Cook It Outdoors* (1941). The dust jacket of the original edition offers considerable insight into the era's gender assumptions about cooking, assuring prospective buyers that it was "a man's book written by a man who understands not only the healthy outdoor eating and cooking habits, but who is an expert at the subtle nuances of tricky flavoring as well." In a follow-up tome co-authored with Helen Brown, *The Complete Book of Outdoor Cookery* (1955), Beard opined, "We believe that [charcoal cookery] is primarily a man's job, and that a woman, if she's smart, will keep it that way."

It is hard to say if Beard's *Cook It Outdoors* inspired the wholesale adoption of the backyard

barbecue, but in 1946 Malcolm LaPrade observed in *That Man in the Kitchen* (subtitled *How to Teach a Woman to Cook*) that men were burning meat in their yards around the country. "In recent years there has been a marked trend toward meat cookery by American men," he wrote. In the suburbs then burgeoning everywhere across the nation, men "formerly content to mow the lawn occasionally . . . have now improvised charcoal-burners or fire-pits on which they grill steaks and hamburgers." The image of Dad in the backyard, eyebrows singed from the overzealous application of charcoal lighter fluid, was on its way to becoming a national icon.

Nor is Dad alone out there. In recent years the traditional Mongolian barbecue of entire oxen, goats, or sheep has spread across China as a demonstration of wealth. The pig roast in Alabama is not so different from the pig roast in Papua New Guinea or Lombardy. Across the world and across the centuries, barbecue has remained a

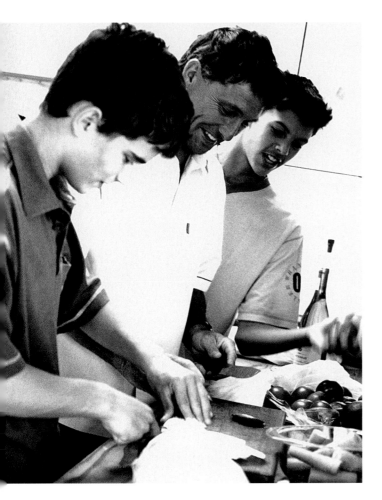

culinary legacy passed from father to son. David Haynes wrote lovingly of his father's mastery of the art in "Chinese Spareribs" in *We Are What We Ate*, a fund-raising book for the hunger-fighting organization Share Our Strength. "Did he have a secret marinade or did he use a special kind of fuel or did he have a separate basting sauce that made his ribs so special? I couldn't begin to tell you. I just know that I am a better man today from having eaten my share of those ribs over all those summers."

It seems American men are most comfortable cooking together. For 150 years the men of Blessed Mother Catholic Church in Owensboro, Kentucky, have spent one night a year in an epic grilling of mutton, chicken, and pork butt for a parish burgoo picnic. In other parts of Kentucky, burgoo is a thick stew of rabbit, squirrel, and whatever other wild game the male cooks find handy. Burgoo suppers often raise money for a new church, school, or other community need.

Soups and stews are part of this male culinary tradition as well. The annual chili cook-offs that began in Texas have spread across the United States. Firemen, policemen, Jaycees, and other male service organizations gather in testosterone-fueled cooking frenzies, all the while expressing strong opinions about which meats and what spices are essential and whether or not beans are allowed. The summertime crawfish, shrimp, and crab boils of Louisiana's Cajun country often take on the same sense of social ritual. The head cook drafts anyone who wanders past to help clean crawfish, chop onions, and stir the stew. Men and boys gather by the pots and the pits to tell jokes, exchange community news, question each other's culinary and sexual proficiency, and sing risqué songs off-key. It's called male bonding.

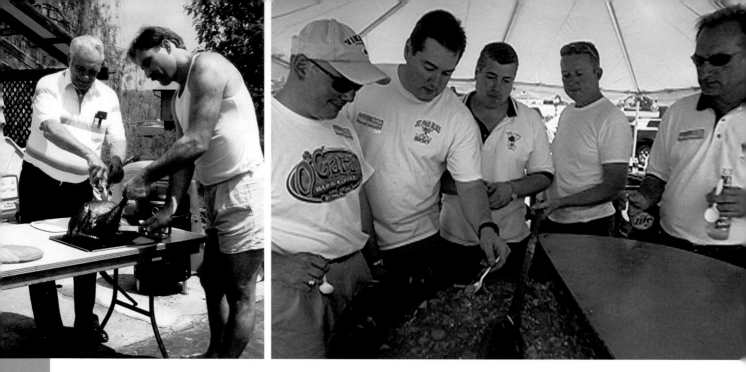

FATHERS AND SONS: BOOYA KINGS

It must be fall in St. Paul, Minnesota, when the men of the community drag out gigantic kettles and pull all-nighters cooking big batches of booya.

The origins of booya, a meat- and vegetable-rich cross between soup and stew, are lost to history. But the mystery only adds to the allure of this hearty dish, which provides warmth and comfort as the cold days of winter approach. Selling cups and even take-home containers of booya is a surefire—and time-honored—way to raise money for a good cause.

One such event is Guns 'n' Hoses, a friendly rivalry between St. Paul police officers and firefighters.

Dick Leitner heads the fire team, following in the footsteps of his father, Bill Leitner Sr., an acknowledged booya master. "I was cooking booyas with my father probably thirty years ago," Dick recalls. "But I got away from it and my brother and his guys down at the bar picked it up after that." His brother, Billy Jr., is the proprietor of Billy's Victorian Bar.

Sitting at the bar beneath a picture of his father, Billy reminisces. "When you said 'booya,' Dad was

ready," says Billy. "I mean he lit up. He'd start getting a little prance in his step because he knew booya was coming—*Now it's time to do it again*. I would say he did well over a hundred booyas in his lifetime. That's a lot of booyas for anybody."

As the weekend for the competition approaches, Dick is confident. "Dad worked with us and showed us how to do it," he says, "so I've been doing it a long time. But I haven't done it consistently every year."

Over at the police station, Tom Radke is handling much of the preparation by himself. "With firefighters, you know what, those guys, they have a lot of manpower," he jokes. "We don't." Tom lops off big heads of cabbage in the field by hand and then drives to Duff's Meats & Deli to pick up his special advance order of oxtails, free-range chicken, beef roasts, center-cut shank meat, and bare knucklebones. Much of the preparatory work of cooking and deboning the meat and chopping the vegetables takes place at the Coffee Cup, a Greek restaurant that's a second home for the cops.

Back with the firefighters, Dick Leitner presides over a crew that peels and chops 120 pounds of potatoes, 100 pounds of onions, 75 pounds of carrots, 50 pounds of rutabagas, and three sacks of cabbages. At noon on Saturday three men help him lift the big black kettles, place them in the back of a pickup truck, and deliver them to the cook-off site in O'Gara's parking lot.

Bill Leitner Sr.'s photo hangs near the cook station. "That is the booya king, my father," Dick says with a cigar clenched between his teeth. "I think he should be present for this. That's how I feel. It's kind of a spiritual thing."

The firefighters start cooking at about 8:00 P.M. Oxtails, which provide the distinctive booya flavor, are tossed into the kettles first. About two dozen cans of beer are added to the mixture—leaving plenty of brews to help the cooks weather the long night.

Tom Radke doesn't arrive with the police kettles until almost midnight. "You're early, you're an hour early," Dick jokes. Now the competition begins in earnest, each side keeping a close eye on the other. They stir the kettles with canoe paddles to keep the booyas from burning. Steam rises in the cold night air.

It's after two o'clock in the morning when a fire truck pulls up with siren blaring. One of Dick's colleagues jumps down and hands him a big packet of seasonings wrapped in cheesecloth. Dick is elated. "This is what it's all about," he says, "the secret spice bag that makes every booya complete." He throws the bag into the kettle and stirs. Booya spice mixtures are traditionally handed down from generation to generation. But Dick admits, "I don't know what's in mine, because my sister won't tell me."

By noon on Sunday both batches of booya are ready and kids stand on the sidewalk holding signs. People crowd around the kettles and taste carefully. "We're trying to be supportive of both," says a young woman, voicing what seems to be a common sentiment.

Even the rivals find kind words for each other. "It's edible this year," Dick Leitner says to Tom Radke. "You're getting there."

"You can walk across that!" Tom rejoins, referring to the thickness of the Leitner recipe.

"I think he'd like this one," Dick says, referring to his dad.

Indeed, the day has brought back fond memories for both Leitner brothers. "I didn't realize it as much until after he was gone, that all the pictures we looked at, Dad always was smiling," says Billy. "Dad was a lot of fun. But then again, it's like anything else. You work hard, you play hard. That describes booya."

ABOVE FROM LEFT TO RIGHT: Bill Leitner Sr., "the booya king," and son Dick. Dick Leitner, on right, tasting booya with the guys (left to right: Dan O'Gara, Tom Radke, John Wegleitner, and Kevin Creamer). Tom Radke and Tommy Theodorakakos at the Coffee Cup.

AMERICAN FAMILY SEASON

Gender roles and family traditions intensify at holidays. While the autumn–winter holiday season sometimes seems to blur together into what Fresno, California, Methodist pastor Pam Abbey once dubbed Hallowthankmas (a three-month "marathon of card-sending, party-throwing, putting up and down decorations, overeating, and overbuying"), it could just as easily be called American Family Season. We gather together for thanks, for worship, for remembrance, for hope . . . and where we gather is around the dining table. However far flung our families have become, we converge for the holidays. In 2004 one American in eight drove, flew, or took a bus or train to be with family or friends for Thanksgiving.

Thanksgiving is our uniquely American holiday, celebrated by presidential proclamation since Abraham Lincoln called for the first national Thanksgiving in 1863. Lincoln spoke to the "blessings of fruitful fields and healthful skies" even in a time of devastation, war, and sacrifice, setting the tone for an annual holiday of thanks for the food we eat and the people we love. Over the years and through a succession of wars, Thanksgiving has come to be the single holiday that gathers the entire American family around the nation's table.

It is a table graced, inevitably, with turkey.

This bird has become so emblematic of the holiday that one-sixth of the turkeys raised in the United States are eaten on the fourth Thursday in November. Many immigrants who arrived in America as children vividly remember the first time they or their siblings managed to cajole their parents into serving turkey at the holiday rather than something more typical of their

homeland. To have a turkey dinner, many recall, meant to be finally "American." Yet apart from turkey and pumpkin pie, Thanksgiving has proved an adaptable feast. In many Italian-American households, for instance, the turkey is almost a side dish to giant pans of lasagna, while some Chinese-American families rub the bird all over with five-spice powder.

Holly Garrison, former food editor at *Parents Magazine,* wrote in *The Thanksgiving Cookbook* that her magazine received more mail and phone calls in November than the rest of the year combined. "Questions ranged from when to start thawing the turkey to instructions for preparing a dish vaguely remembered from childhood." All of these readers, she noted, had one thing in common: "They wanted to re-create at least some of the foods that were served (or they wish had been served) when they were growing up."

Moms and dads—Dad often pitches in to help with the Thanksgiving meal—stuff the birds with the flavors of their family traditions: pecans and corn bread in Appalachia, oysters around the Chesapeake Bay, wild rice in Minnesota, sausage and crawfish in Louisiana. . . . Some families favor whole-berry cranberry sauce, others cranberry jelly. Some serve mashed potatoes, others candied yams. The good china comes out of the storage closet, and the dining room table is set with our best family linens. And so Thanksgiving takes on the ritual meaning of shared values, shared history, good food, and gratitude.

Thanksgiving also has a way of bringing out our most generous spirits. While we may welcome distant relatives at Christmas, Hanukkah, Passover, and Easter, we often share our Thanksgiving tables with friends, neighbors, acquaintances— even strangers—who might otherwise be alone. Moreover, it is the most democratic of holidays. The staples of a traditional Thanksgiving meal are typically so inexpensive that almost every family can afford them. Come Monday morning, when the kids go back to school, rich kids and poor kids alike have enjoyed virtually the same feast.

MOTHERS AND DAUGHTERS: TAMALADA TIME

As Christmas approaches, Bernardina "Nacha" Lucio presides over her daughters and daughters-in-law as they gather in the spacious kitchen of daughter Anna Cruz in San Benito, Texas.

The women are making tamales—a tradition carried on in Mexican and Mexican-American kitchens everywhere. "Tamales are made for an occasion," Diana Kennedy wrote in her book *The Cuisines of Mexico*, "and an occasion is made of making them." As the children decorate the Christmas tree in another room, the women are busy peeling cloves of garlic, chopping pork and other fillings, and kneading the masa, the all-purpose Mexican dough made from stone-ground hominy, lard, and spices.

"A tamalada is a Mexican-American tradition that we inherited from my great-great-grandmother," explains Anna. "It's a gathering of all the family during Christmastime to share family time—and at the same time get together and make tamales."

Belinda Morales, Anna's sister, sums up the importance for the large family. "Christmas wouldn't be the same if we didn't have Grandma's tamales— if we didn't have my mom's tamales and if we didn't make them with her."

Indeed, everyone seems to revolve around Nacha. "My friends call me the tamalada lady because I'm always making tamales," she says with a smile. "We have a great time when we make tamales. Even if it's hard work, being together with my children and family makes me very happy."

A big cooler is filled with water to soften the corn husks that serve as the tamale wrappers. "It's a very inexpensive way to feed a whole bunch of people," says Cindy Puente, another of Anna's sisters. "It's just corn and meat, you know, and it feeds a lot of people for the least amount of money."

A lot of reminiscing goes on as the women prepare the dough and fillings. "My parents were

migrant workers, and so we grew up helping them work in the fields," Anna recalls. "We would travel all the way to Montana and clean sugar beets up there. And then from Montana we would travel to Colorado and we would pick carrots."

The daughters remember their childhood fondly. "In reality, we didn't truly realize that we were poor," Belinda says. "We knew we didn't have what most people had, but we thought we were well off because it was just part of our life. It was routine for us that we migrated, we went to schools in different states, but we were always together."

Nacha was forced to leave school when she was fifteen, and she was adamant that her own children complete their education. Despite some initial resistance from her father, Anna attended college and graduate school, and became a teacher. Now she heads the school district's library system.

"I just had to show my dad my first check stub," she says. "He looked down and shook his head, and

his eyes started watering, and he said, 'You know, Anna, you're making what we never made—all nine of us together working in those fields.' That's when he understood the value of an education."

When all the ingredients are ready, Nacha gives the word and the men join the women in the kitchen to form a tamale-making assembly line. Everyone grabs a big spoon to spread masa on the corn husks and scoop in the fillings. Then they roll the corn husks tight to enclose the mixture. Finally the tamales are layered in a large steamer pot to cook.

The loud buzzing ring of a windup timer announces that the tamales are done. One of the men plucks them from the steamer with tongs. The aroma of masa fills the air, and hungry family members can't resist sampling even before the treats have a chance to cool.

At last the family gathers around a table laden with big platters of tamales. "As my parents are getting older, we know that eventually there is going to come a time where they're not going to be a part of our tamaladas," says Belinda. "So we're cherishing every minute of the tamaladas from here on out. We want to make sure that we remember them and that our children have memories of doing the tamaladas and eating and enjoying each other's company and remembering Grandpa and Grandma."

ABOVE FROM LEFT TO RIGHT: Anna Lucio Cruz spreads masa. The extended Lucio family makes tamales. Family friends Mary Lou Garcia and Elena Trevino help with the preparations.

Tamales

Makes 8 to 9 dozen tamales; allow 3 to 4 tamales per person

For Bernardina Lucio and her family in San Benito, Texas, Christmas is a time to make tamales. It's a labor of love, as generations of women, and now some of the men, get together to happily take part in an old family tradition. Bernardina's daughter, Anna Cruz, shares her mother's recipe.

Boil pork shoulder in the water until tender. Remove the pork from broth and save the broth.

Chop meat into small pieces and place in a large pan. Dissolve chili powder in 1½ cups of the pork broth and then add to the meat. Add cumin, garlic, and salt. Cook and simmer until chili meat is done.

Cream the lard in a mixing bowl. Add masa harina and mix. Add enough of the reserved pork broth to make the dough spreadable with a tablespoon.

Rinse the husks and soak in water for 30 to 45 minutes until pliable. Spread the bottom two-thirds of each husk with 2 tablespoons of the dough. Top with chili meat mix.

To form the tamale, fold the sides of the husk toward the center, making sure the chili meat mix stays in the center, then fold the top down. Pour 2 inches of water into a large pot and arrange the tamales on a rack above the water level. Steam the tamales for about 40 to 50 minutes until cooked. When the tamale can easily slither off the corn husk, it's cooked and ready to eat.

4 pounds pork shoulder

6 cups water

8 tablespoons chili powder

¼ teaspoon cumin

2 medium garlic cloves

Salt to taste

1 pound lard

5 pounds masa harina or 5 pounds masa from a corn tortilla factory

1 package corn husks

Buñuelos

Makes 20 to 25 buñuelos

5 pounds flour

½ teaspoon baking powder

2 teaspoons salt

2 cups shortening

4 cups warm water

Vegetable oil for frying

1 tablespoon ground cinnamon

2 cups sugar

"Buñuelos are to die for!" says Anna Cruz. "Buñuelos are made and eaten during the Christmas season and on New Year's Day. They remind me of my relatives, the first Colunga family who came to America from Mexico to find a better way of life for their children." She loves having them with hot Abuelita Mexican chocolate.

Mix flour, baking powder, and salt in a large bowl. Then add shortening and mix it with the dry ingredients. Add warm water gradually and begin kneading into a dough. Knead for a few minutes, then cover. Let dough rise for approximately 15 minutes in the bowl.

Divide dough into small handsize balls. On a flat countertop or cutting board, roll out each ball of dough with a rolling pin into the shape of a round tortilla about 8 inches in diameter. Then take a fork and prick holes evenly into the tortilla.

Heat about an inch of oil in a 8- or 9-inch frying pan and fry one at a time, flipping the tortilla over until golden brown on both sides.

Remove from pan and place on a paper towel to drain excess oil. Combine the cinnamon and sugar. While the tortillas are still hot, sprinkle the cinnamon sugar on both sides.

Making Merry

Mealtimes at the winter solstice holidays of Christmas and Hanukkah, on the other hand, lend themselves to idiosyncratic family traditions. In Victorian days the proper American Christmas dinner, as enshrined in magazines of the day, revealed an English ancestry: a massive roast beef or goose, mincemeat pie, plum pudding, and hot cider fortified with spices and brandy. Some unkind observers have suggested that the proverbial Christmas fruitcake, leaden with candied fruit and nuts and saturated with spirits, has been passed along—uncut and uneaten—since that Victorian era.

Solstice season eating today may have changed in particulars, but its spirit is still that rosy-cheeked, amber-lit Victorian idyll. Somewhere around Thanksgiving, Auntie makes her list of Christmas cookies to bake, taking note of who will be coming home this year and who won't, adjusting her plans to make some of everyone's favorites—and enough to pack in a tin for the family members posted overseas. Christmas dinner is a time to break out the folding tables and

extra chairs and fret over who sits at the children's table and who graduates to the dining room.

In a sense, none of us has: When we return to our childhood homes for the holidays, we slough off the identities we have worked so hard to achieve and become, once again, our parents' children. As novelist Bobbie Ann Mason wrote in *We Are What We Ate*: "This Christmas my two sisters and my brother and I, along with our families, will head toward home, our real home." She continued, "And what I'm looking forward to

In the Trobriand Islands, an archipelago off the east coast of Papua New Guinea, time itself is reckoned in yam crops: the past crop, two crops back, three crops ahead, and so on. The word for "year," *taytu*, is also the name of a yam species.

most is the green beans and sweet potatoes and creamed corn, the farm fare that once seemed so oppressively ordinary to me."

Because the American workplace comes to a virtual halt for the last two weeks of December, leaving people free to travel, the observance of Hanukkah in the United States often becomes more of an extended-family celebration than it might have been in other societies. Each family's menu is as individual as their Christian neighbors', but fried delicacies are almost always part of the feasts—a solemn remembrance of the oil that burned for a miraculous eight days in the Temple. Families that trace their roots to Central and Eastern Europe almost invariably serve

latkes, while Jews whose families hail from the shores of the Mediterranean might be more likely to enjoy leek fritters.

Apart from the celebratory glass of champagne at midnight that cuts across class and ethnicity in America, our New Year's food customs usually depend on where our ancestors came from. If we're Cuban American, we're likely to eat a dozen grapes at the stroke of midnight, symbolically devouring the last twelve months. If our families come from lands bordering on the Baltic sea, our first bite of the New Year will be herring—fresh or pickled—to ensure good luck for the coming year. If we're Danish, boiled cod will be on the menu for the first meal, for exactly the

same reason. Many different Asian cultures emphasize eating noodles—the longer the better—as either the last meal of the old year or first meal of the new one. They are said to guarantee long life. Many southerners follow the tradition of a dish of hoppin' john (black-eyed peas and rice) on New Year's Day, mindful of the folk saying, *Eat poor on New Year's, eat rich the rest of the year*. Ideally the dish is accompanied by a large heaping of greens—collards, mustard, turnip, kale, or spinach. The color symbolizes folding money. Mexican-American families often start the year with menudo, a stew of tripe and hominy said to cure hangovers and bring health.

Saying Good-Bye

Yet the single event that most often brings our families together—even more than the holidays—is a funeral, especially when it honors the matriarch or patriarch of our clan. We feed our loss with memories and food—and memories *of* food. No sooner does the death notice appear than the doorbell starts ringing as friends and neighbors bring covered dishes of macaroni and cheese or long trays of lasagna, mere spoken condolences being inadequate. In Amish communities the gesture is likely a funeral pie filled with raisins. Mormons often bring a dish called funeral potatoes—hash-browns and cheese baked in a casserole dish—to the bereaved family.

We eat and drink at the wake—ostensibly to awaken the deceased to everlasting life, or simply to remember him or her with good cheer. Anthropologists say that wherever our families come from, the big meals before or after a funeral originated as a way to feed the deceased in the afterlife. The table at a Polish *stypa*, or funeral feast, would always include a dish of peas and noodles prepared with poppy seeds and honey—all ingredients symbolizing eternal life. The English might instead be buried with the ham—an allusion to serving ham at the post-funeral dinner, luncheon, or "funeral tea." Sym-

bolism and cultural legacy aside, we're just as likely to serve Aunt Valerie's favorite *gúlyas* (goulash) recipe at her funeral dinner—or to invite all the mourners to a little restaurant for borscht, roast duck, and blintzes, just like Grandma Sophie would have wanted us to.

FA`A SAMOA

Shortly after World War I, Va`ai Fano was born on the South Pacific island of Samoa, the daughter of a chief. When she passed away eighty years later in Tacoma, Washington, she left four sisters, eleven children, forty-three grandchildren, and thirty-two great-grandchildren.

"She wanted to go back home and visit," recalls daughter Lima Sa`o. Va`ai's illness prevented her from making the 10,000-mile trip. But her family is committed to honoring her with a proper Samoan memorial ceremony—one important phase of respecting Fa`a Samoa, or "the Samoan way."

Va`ai's extended family travels from Samoa, Hawai`i, Kansas City, and California to gather together in Tacoma for three church services and several ceremonial feasts. "The family pitch in, especially the children," explains daughter-in-law Lillian Sa`o. "They each donate some kind of amount of money to take care of all the food and the expenses and everything." The family elders decide how the pooled resources will be spent, and they also plan the menus.

One of Lima's brothers drives from California with a U-Haul truck filled with food—fifty boxes of canned mackerel, six-pound buckets of corned beef (both Samoan favorites), and hundreds of frozen chickens. Taro and bananas also figure prominently in the bounteous feasts.

While young cousins get reacquainted, men and women prepare the food around the clock for five days. They slice taro, peel and cook bananas, cook sausages and chicken, prepare huge pots of chop suey, potato salad, and rice.

At a ceremony at Solid Rock Samoan Church, the youngsters remember their grandmother. "She always taught me that family's always important," says Erlene Schwenke. "Number one: If you go to school, you speak English—you come home, you speak Samoan." Va`ai also impressed upon her family the importance of food as a means of welcome and hospitality. "It is very shameful if you run out of food," explains daughter Lima.

"Samoan funeral is always like this," says Lillian as she pauses from food preparation. "I went to white people's funerals, Oriental funerals. It's just hors d'oeuvres. That is all they have—finger food or doughnuts and coffee. That is a big difference."

At the final burial feast, the ministers are served first. "Those are very important people to us," Lima explains. Traditionally, each honored guest would be presented with a coconut, a symbol of money. But in America, where coconuts are less readily available, the symbol has been modified in an ingenious way that comes across as a gastronomic pun on Coca-Cola. The family presents guests with cans of soda with a dollar bill tucked under the pull tab.

Guests also receive fine woven mats, a traditional sign of wealth, and envelopes of cash. In a ritual of respect and generosity, the guests return some of the gifts to the family members, so that they can give them again. But one thing is certain. No guests go away hungry—and they take several more days' worth of food home with them, neatly wrapped in foil or piled on big platters covered with plastic lids. Sharing food is the most ancient form of giving, and for Va`ai Fano's family it is a form of wealth to be spread throughout the community.

"To us it's very important, it's our mother," says Lima. "And that's our last thing we do for our mother, of our love to her. Whatever you got, you got to give it all."

ABOVE FROM LEFT TO RIGHT: Many ingredients go into a funeral feast. Preparing potato salad for the mourners. Ministers seated at the head table as part of the burial feast and sua ceremony. Relatives share meals together in the days leading up to Va`ai Fano's funeral.

FAMILY RESTAURANT

For more than a century, the ethnic family restaurant has been a place of comfort and familiarity for members of its group—and a bridge to a new life for immigrants coming to the United States. When such places began to open, they were patronized by their own countrymen. But the modern ethnic restaurant is more of a cultural ambassador—welcoming American diners of all backgrounds for a taste of home cooking and a dose of culture. It's also a way for the family to stay together as they get a toehold in a new country. As Marcus Samuelsson observes, the family restaurant is "a common endeavor that ties mother and father, sister and brother together. And the power is in the giving—the giving of love, the giving of food."

"There was always room for family," coffee shop owner Themi Vlahos told *Chicago Greek Circle* magazine in 2002, reminiscing about growing up in one of the restaurants his immigrant father opened after rising from dishwasher to cook to restaurateur. "My mom worked as a waitress. I worked in the business. You created a family. You would go to these Greek-owned restaurants. They had their sons there. They had their daughters there. Why didn't they go work somewhere else? They wanted to stay—it was good to keep everyone together."

Of course, not every family member in every restaurant is keen on staying. The tug-of-war between family ties and a fervent desire to be accepted in the broader world often plays out over food. In writing about "Food as Metaphor," the mother–daughter team of Sheila and Celia Kitzinger observed that "food is a highly charged symbol of relations in families. It is used as a weapon by both children and adults." Food becomes a special battleground as children come of age: "When people reject their culture or their class background, part of that rejection involves repudiating the foods of their childhood." Leaving the family restaurant behind is a way of finding self-definition beyond ethnicity. In the hit movie *My Big Fat Greek Wedding*, thirty-year-old Toula Portokalos has to take computer courses and quit working at Dancing Zorba's to find her beau—and recover her Greek identity in the end. In *Mona in the Promised Land*, novelist Gish Jen's Chinese-American heroine flees the dining room of the family restaurant to embrace suburban Jewish-American culture (and a nice Jewish boy who lives in a tepee).

Ironically perhaps, opening a restaurant that serves cooking from your homeland also turns

out to be a doorway into acceptance in mainstream America today. Chambers of commerce around the country—from immigration hot spots like Raleigh, North Carolina, to cities that attract fewer immigrants, such as Pittsburgh—trumpet the availability of ethnic dining as among their civic attractions.

By the mid-1990s Italian, Mexican, and Cantonese Chinese cuisines were so ingrained that consumers surveyed by the National Restaurant Association no longer identified them as "ethnic." Gnocchi, enchiladas, and pot stickers had become instantly recognizable, perhaps thanks to the Olive Garden, Taco Bell, and tens of thousands of neighborhood Chinese takeout restaurants. By six years later, when the trade group did a second survey, they discovered that Japanese (especially the suddenly ubiquitous sushi), Thai (pad thai), Caribbean (the Cubano sandwich), and Middle Eastern (falafel and hummus) had become so popular that they, too, verged on the familiar. The new ethnic cuisines making a hit with consumers from all walks of life were suddenly Korean and Indian—almost exactly tracking immigration patterns. When someone sits down to a bowl or plate of your food, they get to know you a little better.

FOOD AND SACRIFICE: THE FAMILY BUSINESS

Mingling with her colleagues at the Association of Food Journalists awards ceremony in Boston, Hsiao-Ching Chou is far from her roots in her family's Chinese restaurant in Columbia, Missouri. She nervously twists a ring on her finger as her category—150,000 to 300,000 circulation—is announced.

"The award goes to Hsiao-Ching Chou," says the presenter, *"Seattle Post-Intelligencer."* Hsiao-Ching collects her award and calls her mother even before she leaves the ceremony. "Hi, Mom. I got the first place," she says with pride. "And $300, too."

Although Hsiao-Ching never imagined becoming a food journalist when she was growing up, her career seems almost inevitable in retrospect. Her parents, David and Ellen Chou, met in journalism school in their native Taiwan, and both later studied at the University of Missouri. Her mother worked for Taiwan's Central News Agency in Washington, DC, before the couple put aside some

of their dreams to concentrate on running their own restaurant and raising their family.

Before a visit home for her parents' thirty-second wedding anniversary, Hsiao-Ching visits a Seattle fish market, examines the fresh fish on ice, and selects three red-banded Pacific rockfish to carry with her on the plane. She knows that her visit will revolve around food.

"There's going to be a lot of food, but because I'm going to be home I can help her cook," she says, referring to her mother. "So we're going to make our famous pot stickers, which are better than any you'll ever have at a restaurant."

When Hsiao-Ching reaches her parents' large wood-and-stone house set amid trees, her mother greets her at the door with a big hug. There is, of course, food on the stove. "I made some chicken soup and some noodles for the light snack," Ellen Chou tells her daughter. They head to the kitchen,

lift noodles into their bowls with chopsticks, and then ladle in the broth.

Later, at the restaurant, Hsiao-Ching and her brother Sam eat and reminisce about how their parents got started in the restaurant business. "The version I remember is that there is a big Jesus down in Arkansas," says Sam. "And at the base of the Jesus statue there is an egg roll hut. When my parents came back, they said, 'Well, look, they're selling egg rolls. We could do this.'" Nearly thirty years later Chou's Buffet has become a bustling operation offering a huge array of dishes.

Although running a restaurant has its joys, the never-ending work can take its toll—especially on a family. "Seven days a week we worked," says Hsiao-Ching, who began making wontons when she was eight years old. Sam peeled shrimp, while their baby brother, David, slept in the office above the restaurant. "My mom's hands used to be so creamy white and soft and smooth, and now, after all those years of flipping a wok, she has scars from cuts and burns and her fingers are thick and her wedding rings don't fit anymore."

Even when she returns home for a visit, Hsiao-Ching still feels the tug of duty to the family business. "I have very mixed emotions," she admits. "Because I don't see my family every day anymore. I don't get to talk to my parents every day or have dinner with them. I want to spend this time with them, and not working." She stands at the cash register and places take-out orders in bags. "I feel a responsibility to help out—as much as I don't

ABOVE FROM LEFT TO RIGHT: David and Ellen Chou in the early 1990s. The Chou family and the remnants of the anniversary dinner. Ellen and Hsiao-Ching prepare the dinner. Ginger-scallion shrimp.

want to," she continues. "Because I work during the week and then to come home for a weekend and then work on top of that, it is not fun."

But all hands willingly pitch in to prepare the special menu for the Chous' anniversary celebration: hot and sour soup, pot stickers, ginger-scallion shrimp, honey-roasted duck, asparagus with Chinese black mushrooms, spicy beef with sour greens, and braised red snapper.

All grown up now, youngest brother David mans the restaurant stove with practiced motions, tossing precut meat and vegetables into the wok and shaking them over the fire. "I could do this blindfolded if you asked me," he says. "The bad things are obviously just the workload. I mean, you're here constantly, which is tough. When I was growing up, I couldn't spend time with my friends—couldn't go camping, all those stupid things, you know. But in the end it probably made me a better person."

Family members have come from as far away as Taiwan for the anniversary celebration. Hsiao-Ching's aunt and uncle make a beeline from the airport to the restaurant, then head straight to the kitchen to pitch in making pot stickers.

"Normally when people make them, they buy the prepared dumpling wrappers," says Hsiao-Ching. "That is a nice convenient product, but I am of the firm belief that dumplings ought to be made from scratch because they taste so much better." As her mother flattens the dough with a long, thin rolling pin, Hsiao-Ching scoops up the filling with chopsticks and then carefully crimps the bundles closed.

When all the food is ready, platters and bowls are carried from the kitchen and arrayed on the dining tables. Surrounded by her family and good food, Hsiao-Ching reflects on her heritage and future.

"I think the restaurant was a way to make money, and to afford a home and college educations and cars and clothing and food," she says. "I think it allowed us to be more of a family because we were always together. We worked together, we ate together, we went home together, we came back to work together. My parents, they worked hard so that it could be easier for us."

The evening is bittersweet because the time has come for the Chous to close their business. "They're tired, they need to rest now, and my brother Sam wants to move on with his other business and his life, and for me it will be closure," Hsiao-Ching says.

"Every story has to end, and you have to end one story before you can start another."

ABOVE FROM LEFT TO RIGHT: White peppercorns, an ingredient in pot stickers and hot and sour soup. Eggrolls at Chou's Buffet. Dishes at the anniversary dinner. Fresh red snapper. BOTTOM RIGHT: Hsiao-Ching Chou at age five.

The Chou's Pot Stickers

Makes about 40

2 cups flour (more if needed)

1 cup lukewarm water

2 cups ground pork

2 cups minced Napa (Chinese) cabbage

1 stalk scallion, minced

1 teaspoon minced ginger root

2 tablespoons soy sauce

$1/4$ teaspoon white pepper

1 teaspoon sesame oil

Vegetable oil

For the dough: In a large mixing bowl, combine 2 cups flour and water. Mix well with a dough mixer or wooden spoon until it forms a ball and can be worked with your hands. If the dough feels too wet and sticks to your fingers, work in a couple more tablespoons of flour. The dough should retain some moisture, but it should not be wet. Cover with a damp towel and set aside.

For the filling: Combine pork, Chinese cabbage, scallions, ginger, soy sauce, white pepper, and sesame oil in a bowl. Combine thoroughly with a fork, or work with your hands until well blended.

To form the dumplings: Divide the ball of dough into fourths. Roll each quarter into a log about 5 inches long and $1/2$ inch in diameter. Cut the log into 9 or 10 pieces. Dust with flour as needed.

Roll each piece into a ball, then press it into a silver-dollar-size disk. With a rolling pin (mini-rolling pins work best), roll each disk into a round about 2 inches across.

Place a dollop of filling, about a teaspoonful, in the center of the wrapper. Fold the round so you get a half-moon shape. On the curved edge, pinch the sides together at the midpoint. Hold your thumb and index finger at the midpoint. With your other index finger, push the point of the half moon toward the midpoint and pinch to seal. Pinch the remaining fold to seal. Repeat with the other side, switching hands.

Repeat the rolling and filling steps for each of the remaining dough sections.

Heat a skillet over medium-high heat. Add about 3 tablespoons vegetable oil (enough to coat the bottom with about $1/8$ inch of oil). Place some of the dumplings in the skillet, flat side to the bottom. Brush off any loose flour before placing the dumplings in the skillet. This helps prevent burning.

With the lid in hand, add $1/2$ cup water to skillet and quickly cover, as there will be splattering from the water meeting the hot oil. Cook until the bottoms are golden brown, about 7 to 9 minutes. The sizzling will subside as the water evaporates. Once all the water has boiled off, the pot stickers should be ready. Remove the skillet from heat. Lift the pot stickers out with a spatula. Serve on individual plates or family style.

Serve with a selection of condiments: soy sauce, vinegar, minced fresh garlic, minced scallions, and chili sauce. You can combine any or all of these to taste.

Because every stove and pan is different, the first batch usually becomes the "sacrificial" batch as you figure out just the right temperature and cooking time. But even the bungled pot stickers are tasty.

Hot and Sour Soup

Serves 4

"If you're looking for satisfaction, a bowl of Chinese hot and sour soup is hard to beat," says food writer Hsiao-Ching Chou. "And better yet, it's easy to make. Traditionally, hot and sour soup is made with lily buds, tofulike chunks of curdled pork or duck blood, sautéed slivers of pork, mushrooms, wood ear, bamboo shoot strips, and eggs. The spiciness comes from a combination of white pepper and chili flakes. I prefer hot and sour soup made with only white pepper. In my opinion, versions made with chili sauce have a sweetness and fieriness that throw off the balance of the soup."

To a large soup pot, add water or stock, soy sauce, vinegar, and white pepper. Then add the mushrooms, tofu, wood ear, bamboo shoots, and pork. Let mixture come to a boil.

When soup reaches a boil, turn down heat to medium. In consecutive slow pours, add the cornstarch slurry to the soup while stirring. The soup will start to thicken.

When the soup returns to a boil, drizzle the egg on top. When the egg blossoms, give the soup a gentle stir to incorporate the egg.

Taste the soup. Add more soy, vinegar, and white pepper, if needed. Drizzle with sesame oil and serve with garnishes.

Note: Take a small piece of pork from the loin or chop. Cut into rough strips or little chunks. Sauté in a skillet in 1 tablespoon of vegetable or peanut oil. Add a dash of soy sauce to help it caramelize a little. Cook for about 1 minute, then add to soup.

8 cups water or Chinese-style chicken or pork stock

1/4 cup soy sauce or more to taste

1/4 cup white vinegar or more to taste

2 teaspoons ground white pepper or to taste

4 dried shiitake mushrooms, reconstituted and sliced

1 small block medium or firm tofu, cut into strips

1/2 cup wood ear cut into strips

1/2 cup bamboo shoot strips

1/4 cup pork strips (see note below)

1/4 cup cornstarch, mixed with 1/4 cup water to make a slurry

3 eggs, beaten

Sesame oil

Chopped onions for garnish, optional

Chopped cilantro for garnish, optional

THE TABLE MAKES
THE FAMILY

We have our biological families, and then we have the families that we choose. Some form haphazardly among like-minded friends with whom we grow close. Others we choose with careful deliberation and considerable commitment, as when we enter a religious order.

About 1,400 Roman Catholic monasteries around the world live under a set of rules laid out by St. Benedict around A.D. 530. Writing in a time of great disorder in Christianity, Benedict sought to create religious communities on the model of an extended rural family. His vision stood in contrast to other monastic orders of the early Middle Ages, many of which seemed to compete with each other to eat the least, sleep the least, subject the body to the greatest hardship, and most fully abstain from the comfort of human company. Benedict, in contrast, sought to gather individuals to work, pray, and eat together as a family of faith. His writings pay close attention to meals, from encouraging the working of the land to requiring that the monks all serve in the kitchen in turn. It was likewise important, he

wrote, for the monks to sit down together to dine.

Monks, nuns, and visiting laity have gathered to break bread under the Rule of St. Benedict (as his organizational plan is called) for nearly fifteen centuries now. Benedict's emphasis on the godly calling of agriculture has also given the outside world any number of great cheeses and fine ciders, not to mention the spiced and sweetened liqueur known as Benedictine. Notes chef-author Victor-Antoine D'Avila-Latourrette, himself a monk, "A salad, carefully prepared, is always an occasion of celebration."

Brother Victor-Antoine and his fellow monks sit down to dine in silence—using hand signals to ask for the salt—as one member of the community reads aloud during the meal. The Shakers, a mystical sect of rural Christians who lived monastic lives apart from general society, had their own mealtime rules. Although Shakers ate in silence in the early years of the sect, by the mid–nineteenth century the ban on talking was lifted, and mealtime was set aside for conversation and fellowship.

For Shakers, the dining tables—long and simple affairs, often with bench seating—were manifestations of the Shaker creed that they were all

State with more diners than any other: New Jersey

"Gospel kindred," a form of family more powerful than biological ties. Their food was simple but hearty, and generously seasoned with herbs. Waste was out of the question. You ate what you took; any food left in the kitchen would be served the next day.

Beyond the cloistered walls of the religious community, few institutions are so enshrined among the devout as the church supper. Some church suppers have fixed menus—the baked bean supper, the ham supper—while others are potluck affairs that inadvertently celebrate the diversity of the congregation.

Perhaps the most famous of potluck contributions is the hotdish, a casserole of the Upper Midwest that can be rendered Italian by adding oregano and tomato or Mexican by using tomato soup and chili powder. Without ethnic modifier, the term generally refers to Tater Tot Hotdish, a mixture of hamburger, onion, and cream soup baked with small potato puffs on top. The dish figures prominently in regional comedy, including the reenacted potluck supper at the heart of Brave New Workshop's production of *Minnesota: It's Not Just for Lutherans Anymore* at its two theaters in the Twin Cities.

For many of us the secular counterpart to the church supper is the coffee shop or the diner where we meet and eat with friends. The idea is enshrined in television situation comedy—half the *Seinfeld* shows took place in a restaurant booth, while the characters in *Friends* were

CHICAGO DINER

The White Palace Grill sits on the corner of a busy intersection on Chicago's South Loop. Outside, a large sign announces OPEN 24 HOURS.

Inside, groups of diners sit in red vinyl booths and survey the street scene through the plate glass windows. Solo customers gravitate to the counter, where their swivel-stool perches offer a bird's-eye view of the action at the grill.

"This is really a breakfast place, what they used to call a breakfast joint," says waitress Iris Cruz, who's been working at the diner for a year. "Where you can get breakfast twenty-four hours."

With the ease that comes from eight years of practice, waitress Dorothy Williams threads through the tight space with four plates balanced on her arm. She delivers them to one table and turns to another, pad and paper poised to take an order.

"I love the people," she says when she settles down on one of the counter stools between rushes. "You come in, you talk with them, you know, b.s. with them a little bit. And it's a lot of fun. It's just

like really one big happy family in here."

In her sixteen years at the White Palace, go-go-dancer-turned-waitress Rose Foote has met all kinds of people: "Entertainers, the football stars, the singers, lawyers, doctors," she says. "I mean, we get a conglomerate of people here." Rose thinks that's just fine. "I like the people."

They seem to reciprocate. Dressed in a dark suit and tie, John Tucker sits at a booth to eat his plate of eggs and ham. "I started coming here in 1970," he recalls. "I weighed 172. Now I weigh 272."

Regulars at the White Palace can mark their lives by events that took place in its cozy confines. Ernest Ricks even proposed to his wife, Michelle, over a hearty meal at the White Palace. "It was October 18 when Ernest proposed to me. We were sitting in the second booth in the middle of the window," Michelle recalls in precise detail. "He had a grilled ham-cheese-bacon-scrambled-egg sandwich, and I had a skirt steak, two eggs over easy, hash browns, and wheat toast."

Even on Thanksgiving, when most people sit down to a big meal with family and friends, the diner remains a busy spot. Late in the day the Reverend Walter C. Armstrong strides through the door to sip some coffee and relax among friends. "We fed thirty-nine people today at the house," he tells Rose.

After thirty-three years of patronizing the White Palace, the reverend is set in his ways. "Every time he comes in here, he wants his same seat," Rose explains. "And if you're in that booth, he gets mad!"

Armstrong confirms her observation with a smile. "Many times, if I miss a day, they call and want to know 'What happened to you last night?' " he says. "It's like a family away from home."

ABOVE FROM LEFT TO RIGHT: The White Palace Grill in Chicago. Lori Cantrell serves longtime customer John Tucker. Iris Cruz and Marie Gladie Pagan check an order. BOTTOM RIGHT: Reverend Armstrong and Rose Foote share Thanksgiving wishes.

forever slouching on chairs and couches at Central Perk. The diner is part of our American folklore and our ethos of absolute democracy. Any politician looking for votes—and hoping to take the pulse of the public—will eventually make it to our neighborhood joint for eggs and toast, hash and joe. Those of us who are regulars at such places may gather 'round the Formica counter rather than the family dinner table, but our stool and booth mates are as familiar as kin.

There's good reason why those potatoes are called "home fries." Increasingly, our families are where we find them, and they often coalesce around shared plates, shared tables, and shared experience. Food fuels our daily existence, but it also feeds our minds and comforts our hearts. It is a complex language that speaks about connection and continuity, memory and love, binding us together as families, as communities, and as human beings.

Food, as Marcus Samuelsson concludes at the end of *The Meaning of Food*, "is part of everything we do—as boundless and complex as humanity itself. An old saying goes, 'The stomach is the center and origin of all civilization.' How true!"

Like Marcus, we can all raise a glass to the many people whose personal stories have shed a little light on the large question: *What is the meaning of food?* And we can drink together, as Marcus proposes: "To food! To us!"

ACKNOWLEDGMENTS

As you sow, so shall you reap.

I've always tried to live by this maxim, but let me tell you, the public television combine works exceedingly slowly separating the wheat from the chaff, and *The Meaning of Food* project has been in the making for more than a decade. As you might imagine, over that period scores, probably even hundreds, of people have generously given their expertise, time, encouragement, money, and love to the project and to me personally. And I have been living in dread as to how I will adequately thank all of them given limited time and space, let alone remember everyone's name. But you know who you are. And I thank you all. From the bottom of my heart.

A number of individuals and institutions cannot go without mention.

First, in terms of this book, many thanks are due to my co-authors, Patricia Harris and David Lyon, for their astoundingly well-informed, articulate, and fast work. Wow! *Multi grazie* also to Laura Strom, executive editor for Globe Pequot Press. She somehow made the whole process go smoothly, efficiently, and painlessly. My hearty thanks also go to editor Paula Brisco, prepress coordinator Sue Preneta, designer LeAnna Weller Smith, art director Nancy Freeborn, and researcher Caroline Sherman.

With respect to the overall *Meaning of Food* project, I would like to extend my sincere gratitude to the Corporation for Public Broadcasting, PBS, Unilever/Knorr, Pacific Islanders in Communications, and Humanities Washington Documentary Pooled Fund for the financial support that made it all possible. A special thanks to Cheryl Head of CPB and Annie Moriyasu of PIC, two individuals without whose steady encouragement and enthusiasm the project would not have survived. Thanks also to my sister and brother-in-law, Christine McLaughlin and Ofer Gneezy, for kicking in some well-timed funds during research and development just when the pot was running perilously low.

Kudos also to Oregon Public Broadcasting, our fiscal sponsor and liaison to the PBS system. As an independent producer, I have worked with a number of PBS stations, and although the relationship is inevitably fraught with difficulties, this was the smoothest ride I've had so far. Much credit to Executive Producer Dave Davis, who was a steadfast ally, supporter, and all-around decent guy, along with Director of Production John Booth and the rest of the OPB team for their friendly professionalism.

A big thanks goes to Marcus Samuelsson for being interested in the project (even when he had no idea who we were) and for being so even-keeled, amiable, and professional.

Many of the key players on this series' production team were my long-term friends and colleagues. Thankfully, surprisingly, most of us are still talking to each other! Karin Williams and Vivian Kleiman, senior producers and directors, were involved nearly from the beginning. With their long résumés in documentary and TV production, they both contributed invaluable expertise and wisdom. Also important was our shared sense of gluttony: Karin and I always brainstormed best over coffee and chocolate at Seattle's Macrina Bakery, and Vivian and I shared many a fine Indian snack at Vik's Chaat Corner in Berkeley. In our most glorious moment, the three of us were treated to an exquisite lunch by Alice Waters at Chez Panisse. There's no better way to get the creative juices flowing.

Series producer Maria Gargiulo, though a newcomer to the party, immediately pitched in with

energy, verve, and an impressive talent for regularly making homemade cakes and pies for the staff. Steve Kodish, coproducer and production manager, was a one-man band who served as HR, IT, and PR departments rolled into one individual, on top of being keeper of the Big Bad Budget. Not to mention a pretty mean lasagna chef! Shannon Gee was another rock shoring up production. Serving as both producer and postproduction supervisor, she successfully shifted gears from developing stories and cajoling show characters to running herd over hundreds of tapes and complicated technical specifications. Plus she maintained the ever-crucial supply of wasabi pea snacks. Though the youngest member of the team, producer Kimberlee Bassford was invariably the calmest, best prepared, and best organized. Her professionalism was much appreciated, as was the cooler of Local Food she brought back to the office from her native Hawai`i. Smooth-talking producer John Mikulenka is reputed to be able to talk blood from a stone, a crucial talent in documentary production. Although he claimed no ethnic food heritage of his own, once his Texas Czech roots were discovered, it was clear that—even though John remained the token White Office Male—he wasn't as bland as he put on.

Longtime friend and colleague Susan Kim (my first boss in television) wrote most of the script, cheerfully putting up with a certain amount of disorganization and early lack of focus. Greg Palmer, also a longtime friend and colleague, wrote a significant portion of the early show treatments, and was one of the few people always willing to pitch in, even when the remuneration wasn't yet flowing. For that I remain forever grateful.

Many other people willingly committed their blood and sweat to the project, among them associate producers Marina Gordon, Mimi Wong, Laurie Bohm, and Rosalyn Brandon; editors Bob de Maio, Jill Friedberg, Michael Cross, Kris Kristensen, and Drew Keller; our wonderful director of photography and drinking buddy, Diana Wilmar; our wonderful graphic designer, Lisa Moore; our also wonderful composer, Stephen Cavit; and scores of interns (thank you Lindsay, Andrew, Lena, Massimo, and Kamer, among others). All this is not to mention the extraordinary individuals who allowed us to come into their lives and families and videotape their private moments. Thank you!

My gratitude also goes out to all of our project advisers, particularly Dr. Sidney Mintz, professor emeritus of Johns Hopkins University, who put up

with me hassling him about this project since its inception (provoking him to call me at one point a "charming nudge"), and Dr. Miriam Kahn of the University of Washington, who remained graciously supportive and interested no matter the project's ups and downs. Also, I very much appreciate and am eternally impressed by the time and care Alice Waters of Chez Panisse—along with her wonderful colleagues Cristina Salas-Poras and Sylvan Brackett—took with the project. That such major bigwigs in the food world were willing to read and respond in detail to our show treatments, and to always get back to us no matter how silly our questions, reveals exceeding kindness and generosity.

On a personal note, I remain eternally grateful to all my friends and family who put up with me nattering on about this project for more than a decade. Thanks to Margaret Rogers for being so flexible. A huge thanks to my husband, Jeff Teitelbaum, for being such a good guy: filling in wherever needed as cheerleader, sounding board, cook, technical adviser, and/or associate producer. And finally thanks to my mom and dad, Billie and John McLaughlin. My mom's love of food and background as a professional home economist are really what gave me the inspiration for this project. My dad, who was constantly mysti-

fied by the vagaries of independent documentary production and by the fact I didn't work regular hours at a regular office, did not live to see this project completed. In his later years one of his ailments was congestive heart failure, a condition my family assumed had been brought on by a single helping of Mom's corned beef and cabbage—a theory corroborated by the doctor. Dad was never again allowed to have corned beef and cabbage, one of his favorite meals. So Dad, here's to you. I hope you're out there somewhere, eating all the corned beef and cabbage, with banana cream pie, that you want, amazed and proud that this project finally really happened.

As one of the people in the series, Hsiao-Ching Chou, says, "Every story has to end, and you have to end one story before you can start another."

May we all go on to new stories and new projects that are fabulous and rewarding in and of themselves, but that also continue and enrich the old stories in exciting and unexpected ways.

—SUE McLAUGHLIN

A WORLD OF TASTE: MARCUS SAMUELSSON

Marcus Samuelsson, host of *The Meaning of Food* on PBS, believes that what makes food universal "is that it's a very quick way of explaining who you are, where you came from, what you like. Almost wherever you are, you can talk about your own culture, your own experience through food."

If so, then Samuelsson is a citizen of the world. Born in Ethiopia in 1970, he was orphaned at the age of three and adopted by a couple from Göteborg, Sweden. He grew up on the west coast of Sweden, a period he remembers as an idyllic time spent with family and close friends.

"I loved picking mushrooms and berries with my family," Samuelsson recalls. "Sometimes, we'd go fishing. Then my grandmother Helga would make us some very Swedish food—mushroom stew on toast, pancakes, and blueberry soup." It was at the side of his grandmother, herself a professional cook, that Samuelsson discovered his passion for the kitchen.

"I may be a professional chef, but my love of cooking comes straight from my family," he says. "For me, food and family have always been deeply connected. My grandma's cooking is very much the base and foundation of how I cook today."

As a teenager, his culinary training shifted south when he secured a position at a three-star Michelin restaurant in France. Today Samuelsson is executive chef and co-owner of two restaurants in New York: Aquavit, which offers innovative interpretations of classic Scandinavian cuisine by marrying tradition with contemporary ideas, and Riingo, a Japanese-American fusion restaurant. He is also an ambassador for UNICEF.

Among his many accolades, Samuelsson was the youngest chef ever to receive a three-star restaurant review from *The New York Times*; restaurant critic Ruth Reichl awarded the designation in 1995. In May 2001 Aquavit was awarded another three-star review from *Times* critic William Grimes. In 2003 Samuelsson was chosen Best Chef in New York City by the James Beard Foundation. He was also named one of the Great Chefs of America by the Culinary Institute of America.

"Food is important to me because feeding people is my job," Samuelsson muses. "And like everybody I know, I love to eat. But food is much more than that. It's powerfully symbolic and complex. To cook something, to serve it, to share it with others—each is far more meaningful than just a job, a pleasure, or even a necessity. Through food, we express love. We bring comfort and hope. We forge new relationships, and reinforce old bonds.

"Food reaffirms not only our humanity, but the joy of being alive."

BIBLIOGRAPHY

Ackerman, Diane. *A Natural History of the Senses.* New York: Random House, 1990.

Allen, Stewart Lee. *In the Devil's Garden: A Sinful History of Forbidden Food.* New York: Ballantine Books, 2002.

Ancelet, Barry J., Jay D. Edwards, and Glen Pitre. *Cajun Country.* Jackson: University Press of Mississippi, 1991.

Beard, James M. *Cook It Outdoors.* New York: M. Barrows & Co., 1941.

———. *Fowl and Game Cookery.* New York: M. Barrows & Co., 1944.

———. *Hors d'Oeuvre and Canapés.* New York: M. Barrows & Co., 1940.

Beard, James M., and Helen Brown. *The Complete Book of Outdoor Cookery.* New York: Doubleday, 1955.

Brown, Linda Keller, and Kay Mussell, eds. *Ethnic and Regional Foodways in the United States: The Performance of Group Identity.* Knoxville: University of Tennessee Press, 1984.

Camporesi, Piero. *Bread of Dreams: Food and Fantasy in Early Modern Europe.* Translated from the Italian by David Gentilcore. Chicago: University of Chicago Press, 1989.

Chalmers, Irena. *The Great Food Almanac.* San Francisco: Collins Publishers, 1994.

Columbus, Christopher. *The Log of Christopher Columbus.* Translated from the Spanish by Robert F. Fuson. Camden, Maine: International Marine Publishing, 1987.

Counihan, Carole, and Penny Van Esterik, eds. *Food and Culture: A Reader.* New York: Routledge, 1997.

D'Avila-Latourette, Brother Victor-Antoine. *Twelve Months of Monastery Salads.* Boston: Harvard Common Press, 2004.

De Silva, Cara, ed. *In Memory's Kitchen: A Legacy from the Women of Terezín.* Translated from the Czech and German by Bianca Steiner Brown. New Jersey and London: Jason Aronson, Inc., 1996.

Esquivel, Laura. *Between Two Fires: Intimate Writing on Life, Love, Food & Flavor.* Translated from the Spanish by Stephen Lytle. New York: Crown Publishers, 2000.

———. *Like Water for Chocolate: a novel in monthly installments, with recipes, romances, and home remedies.* Translated from the Spanish by Carol Christensen and Thomas Christensen. New York: Doubleday, 1992.

Farb, Peter, and George Armelagos. *Consuming Passions: The Anthropology of Eating.* Boston: Houghton Mifflin Company, 1980.

Fisher, M. F. K. *The Gastronomical Me.* New York: North Point Press, 1943, 1954.

———. *Serve It Forth.* New York: North Point Press, 1937, 1954.

Flandrin, Jean-Louis, and Massimo Montanari, eds. *Food: A Culinary History from Antiquity to the Present.* New York: Columbia University Press, 1999.

Gabaccia, Donna R. *We Are What We Eat: Ethnic Food and the Making of Americans.* Cambridge, Mass., and London: Harvard University Press, 1998.

Garrison, Holly. *The Thanksgiving Cookbook.* New York: MacMillan Publishing Company, 1991.

Haber, Barbara. *From Hardtack to Home Fries: An Uncommon History of American Cooks and Meals.* New York: The Free Press, 2002.

Haberstein, Robert W., and William M. Lamers. *Funeral Customs the World Over.* Milwaukee: Bulfin Printers, revised edition 1973.

Hemingway, Ernest. *The Sun Also Rises*. New York: Charles Scribners Sons, 1926, 1954.

Jen, Gish. *Mona in the Promised Land*. New York: Alfred A. Knopf, 1996.

Jones, Evan. *American Food: The Gastronomic Story*. Woodstock, N.Y.: The Overlook Press, 1990.

Kahn, Miriam. *Always Hungry, Never Greedy: Food and the Expression of Gender in a Melanesian Society*. Cambridge: Cambridge University Press, 1986.

Kame`eleihiwa, Lilikala. *Native Land and Foreign Desires*. Honolulu: Bishop Museum Press, 1992.

Kass, Leon. *The Hungry Soul: Eating and the Perfecting of Our Nature*. New York: Free Press, Maxwell Macmillan Canada, 1994.

Kennedy, Diana. *The Cuisines of Mexico*. New York: Harper & Row, revised edition 1986.

Kirlin, Katherine S. *Smithsonian Folklife Cookbook*. Washington, D.C.: Smithsonian Institution Press. 1991.

LaPrade, Malcolm. *That Man in the Kitchen: How to Teach a Woman to Cook*. Boston: Houghton Mifflin Company, 1946.

Laudan, Rachel. *The Food of Paradise: Exploring Hawaii's Culinary Heritage*. Honolulu: University of Hawai`i Press, 1996.

Lévi-Strauss, Claude. *The Raw and the Cooked*. Translated from the French by John and Doreen Weightman. New York: Harper & Row, 1969.

MacClancy, Jeremy. *Consuming Culture*. London: Chapman, 1992.

Malinowski, Bronislaw. *The Sexual Life of Savages in North-Western Melanesia*. New York: Harcourt, Brace, 1929.

Messerli, Douglas, ed. *The Sun & Moon Guide to Eating Through Literature and Art*. Los Angeles: Sun & Moon Press, 1994.

Mintz, Sidney W. *Sweetness and Power: The Place of Sugar in Modern History*. New York: Viking, 1985.

——. *Tasting Food, Tasting Freedom: Excursions Into Eating, Culture, and the Past*. Boston: Beacon Press, 1996.

Pillsbury, Richard. *No Foreign Food: The American Diet in Time and Place*. Boulder, Colo.: Westview Press, 1998.

Pliny the Elder. *Natural History: A Selection*. Translated from the Latin by John Healy. London: Penguin Classics, 1991.

Reichl, Ruth. *Tender at the Bone*. New York: Random House, 1998.

Root, Waverly, and Richard de Rochemont. *Eating in America: A History*. New York: William Morrow and Company, 1976.

Rozin, Elisabeth. *Ethnic Cuisine: The Flavor-Principle Cookbook*. Lexington, Mass.: Stephen Greene Press, 1983.

Shapiro, Laura. *Perfection Salad: Women and Cooking at the Turn of the Century*. New York: Farrar, Strauss and Giroux, 1986.

——. *Something from the Oven: Reinventing Dinner in 1950s America*. New York: Viking Penguin, 2004.

Sokolov, Raymond. *Why We Eat What We Eat*. New York: Summit Books, 1991.

Theroux, Paul. *The Happy Isles of Oceania: Paddling the Pacific*. New York: Ballantine Books, 1992.

Winegardner, Mark, ed. *We Are What We Ate: 24 Memories of Food*. San Diego, Calif.: Harcourt Brace, 1998.

INDEX

A

abstinence, 33, 34, 35
African cooking, 19-21, 91
American cuisine, 88-105
American restaurants, 102-5
animals, 41-42, 44, 79
Annakuta, 40
aphrodisiac, 32, 87
asparagus, 32
Axel, Richard, 5-6
Aztecs, 42, 44

B

barbecue, 118-19
Baum, Joe, 102
Beard, James, 102, 103, 117
biryani, 63
booya, 120-21
bread, 45, 62, 65, 70, 83
breakfast, 150-51
Brillat-Savarin, Jean-Anthelme, 5, 6, 62
Buck, Linda, 5-6
buñuelos, 130
burgoo, 119

C

caffeine, 32
Cajun cooking, 91, 119
cake, 1-2, 23, 28, 48
California cuisine, 103
Cantonese cooking, 96

Caplan, Frieda, 105
Caribbean cooking, 78
Casanova, Giacomo, 32
Catholics, 35, 42, 148
cattle, 78
charcoal cooking, 116, 117-18
Chez Panisse, 102-3
Child, Julia, 102
chile peppers, x, 12, 96
chili, 119
China, 50-51, 62-63, 73
Chinese cooking, 70, 140-43
Chinese New Year, 96
chitlins, 78
chocolate, 32-33
Christianity, 33, 35, 42, 45, 86
Christmas, 83, 126-29, 130, 132-34
church suppers, 149
coffee cake, 56, 83
Columbus, Christopher, 73, 83-84
comfort food, 43, 101
concentration camps, 46-49
contraband food, 14-15
convenience foods, 112-13
cookbooks, 112, 114, 116
corn, 73-74
couscous, 70
cravings, 33
Creole cooking, 91
cuisine, American, 88-105
culinary schools, 103, 112
Czechoslovakia, 46-48, 92-95

D

dates, 37
Day of the Dead, 51, 53

death, 43, 50-53, 135
dietary laws, 85-86
diners, 148, 149-52
dinner, 110
domestic science, 88, 112
durian, 9, 87

E

Egyptians, 50
Eid, 37
endorphins, 12
erotic food, 23, 27-28, 32-33
Escoffier, Auguste, 103
Esquivel, Laura, 28, 35, 40, 50
eternal food, 50-53
ethnicity, 96-99, 138-39, 140-43

F

Fa`a Samoa, 136-37
family restaurants, 138-39, 140-43
Farmer, Fannie Merritt, 112
fasting, 18, 33-35, 36-37
feasts, 6, 17, 23, 24-25, 44, 137
fertility, 23, 30, 32
festivals, 40, 44, 45, 50-51, 96, 97, 99
fidelity, 70
Fisher, M. F. K., 2
flan, 53